Charles William Leverett Johnson

Musical Pitch and the Measurement of Intervals Among the Ancient Greeks

Charles William Leverett Johnson

Musical Pitch and the Measurement of Intervals Among the Ancient Greeks

ISBN/EAN: 9783744743259

Printed in Europe, USA, Canada, Australia, Japan

Cover: Foto ©Thomas Meinert / pixelio.de

More available books at **www.hansebooks.com**

MUSICAL PITCH

AND

THE MEASUREMENT OF INTERVALS

AMONG THE ANCIENT GREEKS

BY

CHARLES W. L. JOHNSON, Ph. D.

+

THESIS

PRESENTED FOR THE DEGREE OF DOCTOR OF PHILOSOPHY

IN THE JOHNS HOPKINS UNIVERSITY

+

BALTIMORE

1896

PREFACE.

The present dissertation, originally submitted to the authorities
in April, 1895, is now printed in conformity with the University
regulations. I have thought it best to avail myself of the opportunity thus offered to make a number of changes and to expand
the treatment in certain directions. Karl von Jan's *Musici Scriptores Graeci* (Bibliotheca Teubneriana, 1895), which appeared too
late to be of service in the original preparation of the thesis, has
been used for the quotations from the Aristotelian *Problems* and
from the works of Euclid, Nicomachus, Gaudentius, and Bacchius.
Aristoxenus is quoted from the edition of Westphal (Vol. II, edited
by F. Saran, Leipsic, 1893). The pages of Meibomius, *Antiquae
Musicae Auctores Septem*, Amsterdam, 1652, are, however, retained
in making citations from the authors embraced in this work.
For the musical treatises of Claudius Ptolemy, Porphyry, and
Bryennius the only available text was that which is found in the
third volume of John Wallis's *Opera Mathematica*, Oxford, 1699.
I take pleasure in acknowledging my 'great obligation to the
authorities of the Boston Athenaeum for their courtesy in per-
mitting me to consult this rare work at leisure in my own home.
I am also indebted for the opportunity accorded me while in
England in 1894 to use the copies of Wallis and Meibomius
belonging to the Cambridge University Library.

CHARLES W. L. JOHNSON.

BALTIMORE, *December*, 1896.

TABLE OF CONTENTS.

MUSICAL PITCH

AND

THE MEASUREMENT OF INTERVALS AMONG THE ANCIENT GREEKS.

THE material available for reconstructing the music of classical antiquity is unfortunately not very abundant. In the case of the other fine arts, it is possible for the modern world actually to realize the art of the ancients through the monuments of their activity which have survived to our day. This is preëminently the case with the three great space-arts, sculpture, architecture, and painting. We are able to obtain an immediate appreciation of these arts by actual contemplation of sculptural, architectural, and pictorial remains, and the extent of our appreciation will depend on the degree to which, from the nature of the material used, these remains have been able to withstand the destructive agencies of time and the elements. In this way those arts in which stone was so generally the material employed have fared better than those in which a less durable medium was used. We may compare architecture and sculpture with painting and the ceramic art in this matter. But in all of them the appreciation is immediate; the contact between the ancient and the modern world is direct. It is possible to study the actual creations of ancient art, and it is not necessary to rely wholly or even partly on indirect means of approach, like theoretical treatises and chance allusions in literature.

1

How different is the state of affairs in the case of the time-arts, poetry and music! Although it is self-evident, it is interesting to reflect that these arts, based as they are on a medium so immaterial as sound, demand a fresh representation whenever it is desired actually to experience any of their productions; and this is true no less of poetry than of music, although certain qualifications must be added in the case of the former. For when we read to ourselves, the reproduction of the sounds is, of course, imagined, and reading music differs from reading language only in that it is an art more difficult to acquire, and that less satisfactory results are obtained in the silent reading of music than in that of written words. It follows that the fullest appreciation of these time-arts can be gained only when we are able to reproduce the actual sounds with at least approximate accuracy.

But poetry stands on an entirely different plane from music for an evident reason. It is that poetry does not consist of words alone, however melodious and rhythmical, but the thought is an essential element in its composition; and if it is objected that this is true of music also, it is true in quite a different sense. Musical sounds are not, individually, like works, the symbols of thoughts, but the thought in music arises from the combination and union of sounds, but *is not* the sounds, while in language the thought of a sentence springs from the combination of lesser thoughts, of which the words are only the symbols, and for which any other symbols, like signs with the fingers, could serve almost as well.

For these reasons poetry is in a far better position than music for perpetuating its productions. To take the case of Greek poetry, we are able to lay down with no little confidence rules for the correct pronunciation of the words, and for the correct scansion of the metres. But even if by some means not now available we should learn that all our suppositions on these points were utterly wrong, we should still possess the thought, and the thought is imperishable so long as a knowledge of the language exists. The written word is not a bad substitute for the spoken word. But in the case of music there is no element which we can separate, or imagine to be separated, from the sounds themselves, without destroying the very nature of the music. While rhythm is, perhaps, after the sounds, *i. e.*, the pitch element in sounds, the most important constituent, rhythm alone is not music.

In what condition, then, is the study of ancient classical music with regard to our ability to reproduce the actual sounds? What are the steps which we must take in order to obtain a correct interpretation of the music of the Greeks?

From one point of view musical sounds may be regarded as endowed with two dimensions. One of these is pitch; the other is time. Every sound in a melody differs from every other sound, either in one of these dimensions or in both; and every sound is defined, or at least is defined in every particular essential to constituting the melody, by giving the pitch of each note and its time-element in the two respects of the position in time and the duration in time. The time-coördinates and the pitch-coördinates together constitute the melody. As a result, melody can be represented graphically on a plane, and this is what is done in a rough way by the ordinary staff notation by means of the position of the notes *on* the staff (modified by the key-signature and the 'accidental' sharps and flats), and by their position *along* the staff (as determined by the bars and modified by differences in their appearance to give their duration).

There are, to be sure, other ways in which musical notes may differ from one another. In addition to differences of pitch and of duration, we may have differences of 'timbre' or 'quality,' and differences in the loudness or 'force' with which the notes are sounded. But the quality and the force may be varied without destroying the nature of a melody, whereas alterations in the pitches of the notes which form a tune, and in their duration-values, cannot, in general, be made without altering the melody. It is only when the changes of pitch or of duration are uniform throughout a piece of music that a melody may be said to remain the same. In the one case we have the familiar phenomenon of a change of key; in the other, a change of the 'tempo,' *i. e.*, the speed with which the music is performed. In both, the notes bear the *same relation* to one another as before; there has been a change in the absolute values alone. But in general it is true that the pitches and durations are essential, while the quality and loudness are accidental, in the formation of melodies. We cannot replace a note of one pitch by a note of another, nor change the rhythm by lengthening or shortening notes at pleasure without affecting the nature and character of the tune.[1]

If now the problem is presented to the student of ancient music to reproduce the sounds of any piece of that music for which we are so fortunate as to possess the written notes, the most important points to be determined will be the pitches of the notes and their differences in duration. We may safely leave such matters as the right degrees of loudness and softness, and the element of speed or the tempo to our own taste. The quality of the tones will depend on the character of the music, whether vocal or instrumental, and if instrumental, we must rely on our knowledge of ancient musical instruments. But the rhythm and the melody (in narrower sense) are matters of primary importance.

There is a very considerable difference, however, in the difficulty of determining the exact equivalents for the symbols

---

[1] It is not intended in the above statement to assert that rhythm is independent of loudness, for rhythm is based on the recurrence of a stress at equal intervals of time. But inasmuch as, in music if not in poetry, that sound which from its position would ordinarily bear the stress may *part with its stress* in favor of a succeeding note, or may be *altogether absent*, it would seem that the stress feature of rhythm was *derived* from the sequence of long and short durations of the notes, *i. e.*, from their metre, taken in connection with the pitch of the notes (in the case of music). In other words, if a tune is played absolutely without stress, the time will manifest itself in spite of all through the character of the tune. But, be this as it may, if the reader will exclude stress from the term loudness, the statement will stand.

used to denote pitch, and for those used to mark the rhythm. In fact in most of the known remains of Greek music, the rhythm is left to be determined by the metre of the words to which the music was sung. It will moreover readily be admitted that errors in the interpretation of the rhythm would not result in so thorough a misunderstanding as would errors in the translation of the pitch-values of the ancient notes.

The first step in this important determination of the pitch-values may well be to discover the order or succession of the notes in the matter of acuteness and graveness. The next would then be to ascertain the exact distances at which the notes stand with reference to one another. As to the mere order of the notes, several of the ancient treatises supply us with this information, but when the notes are enumerated *by name* alone and not by written symbol, we must still obtain a correspondence between the written notes and their names. This we are able to do by means of the diagrams which are found in the invaluable work of Alypius, and in the works of Gaudentius and Bacchius Senior. By means of this information alone we could plot a curve of any ancient melody, such that every rise and fall in pitch was represented, and only the amount of this motion would remain undetermined. The second step supplies this deficiency. We ascertain for each note the distance or interval at which it stands from its neighbors. This done, we are in possession of all the *knowledge* necessary to reproduce the sounds denoted by the ancient notation. Our ability to *translate* the notation correctly into the modern notation, and to reproduce the sounds vocally or instrumentally, will, of course, depend for the most part on the similarity of the music in question to modern music.

The present dissertation is concerned with this second step, and is an attempt to show to what extent our knowledge of the absolute width of musical intervals in general among the Greeks is based on firm foundations. No attempt is made to show what are the modern equivalents for the actual notes employed in their music, nor to establish the width of the corresponding intervals in connection with their occurrence in actual melody and in the ancient scales. The subject is the measurement of intervals abstractly considered, irrespective of their place in the scale and irrespective of their function in actual representation. Pitch is consequently considered, not as a quality or property of musical sounds, but as a quantity, which may be measured like any other quantity. And in its measurement we are not concerned so much with the absolute position of notes on the scale of acuteness and graveness, as with their relative position. Since pitch lengths can be measured only when the bounds are rigidly fixed, a discussion of the musical sound will precede, involving a few words on the classification of sounds and the place therein of musical sounds and on the ancient conception of pitch.

The ancient explanations of sound as a physical phenomenon, however insufficient from a modern point of view, are accurate enough in general for musical purposes. The important part played by the air, either as the cause of sound or as the medium of its transmission to our ears, seems to have been very universally recognized. Plato [1] defines sound as a "stroke transmitted through the ears by the air and passed through the brain and the blood to the soul." That a blow is necessary for the production of a sound seems to have been brought out before the time of Archytas, for Archytas approves of this doctrine of his predecessors in a passage quoted by Porphyry in his *commentarius ad Ptolemaeum*, p. 236 Wallis (Wallis, *Opera Mathematica*, III. p. 236).[2] But, according

---

[1] *Timaeus*, XXIX. 67 B: ὅλως μὲν οὖν φωνὴν θῶμεν τὴν δι' ὤτων ὑπ' ἀέρος ἐγκεφάλου τε καὶ αἵματος μέχρι ψυχῆς πληγὴν διαδιδομένην. The translation is from Mr. Archer-Hind's Edition of the *Timaeus*. See the notes on this passage and on 80 A (pages 246 and 300).

[2] The passage is quoted by K. von Jan, *Musici Scriptores Graeci* (1895), p. 131: καλῶς μοι δοκοῦντι τὸ περὶ τὰ μαθήματα διαγνῶναι . . . περί τε δὴ τᾶς τῶν ἄστρων ταχυτᾶτος . . . καὶ περὶ γαμετρίας καὶ ἀριθμῶν, καὶ οὐχ ἥκιστα περὶ μουσικῆς . . . πρᾶτον μὲν οὖν ἐσκέψαντο, ὅτι οὐ δυνατόν ἐστιν εἶμεν ψόφον μὴ γενηθείσας πληγᾶς τινων ποτ' ἄλληλα. (See Mullach, *Fragm. Philos. Gr.* I. p. 564.)

to K. von Jan,[1] Archytas did not attribute sound to movement of the air, but only regarded the visible movement of the sounding instrument, to produce which a blow is necessary.

The views of Aristotle can best be seen from the passages collected by von Jan.[2] Aristotle too lays stress on the importance of a blow (de anima, II 8, 2: πληγὴ γάρ ἐστιν ἡ ποιοῦσα), but the part played by the air is brought out (ibid. 3: δεῖ στερεῶν πληγὴν γενέσθαι πρὸς ἄλληλα καὶ πρὸς τὸν ἀέρα), and sound is declared to be an actual movement of the air (ibid. 9: ἀέρος κίνησίς τίς ἐστιν ὁ ψόφος).[3] The nature of the movement is shown in the words (ibid. 6), ὅταν δὲ (ὁ ἀὴρ) κωλυθῇ θρύπτεσθαι, ἡ τούτου κίνησις ψόφος, and (3) τοῦτο δὲ γίνεται, ὅταν ὑπομένῃ πληγεὶς ὁ ἀὴρ καὶ μὴ διαχυθῇ. This definition reappears in Theon of Smyrna, de musica, 6 (p. 50 Hiller), in a quotation from Adrastus: φησὶ δὲ καὶ τοὺς Πυθαγορικοὺς περὶ αὐτῶν οὕτω τεχνολογεῖν· ἐπεὶ μέλος μὲν πᾶν καὶ πᾶς φθόγγος φωνή τίς ἐστιν, ἄπασα δὲ φωνὴ ψόφος, ψόφος δὲ πλῆξις ἀέρος κεκωλυμένου θρύπτεσθαι (quoted also by Bryennius, p. 394 Wallis), and in Nicomachus, harmonices manuale, 4, p. 7 Meib.: καθόλου γάρ φαμεν ψόφον μὲν εἶναι πλῆξιν ἀέρος ἄθρυπτον (or ἀθρύπτου) μέχρι ἀκοῆς.

A fuller explanation of the phenomenon of sound is given in the tract de audibilibus, attributed to Aristotle.[4]

Aristotle, de audib., p. 800 a, Bekker: τὰς δὲ φωνὰς ἁπάσας συμβαίνει γίγνεσθαι καὶ τοὺς ψόφους ἢ τῶν σωμάτων ἢ τοῦ ἀέρος πρὸς τὰ σώματα προσπίπτοντος, οὐ τῷ τὸν ἀέρα σχηματίζεσθαι, καθάπερ οἴονταί τινες, ἀλλὰ τῷ κινεῖσθαι παραπλησίως αὐτὸν συστελλόμενον καὶ ἐκτεινόμενον καὶ καταλαμβανόμενον, ἔτι δὲ συγκρούοντα διὰ τὰς τοῦ πνεύματος καὶ τῶν χορδῶν γιγνομένας πληγάς. ὅταν γὰρ τὸν ἐφεξῆς ἀέρα πλήξῃ τὸ πνεῦμα τὸ ἐμπῖπτον αὐτῷ, ὁ ἀὴρ ἤδη φέρεται βίᾳ,

---

[1] K. von Jan, op. cit., p. 135. See, however, p. 43, l. 22.

[2] K. von Jan, op. cit., p. 3, sq.

[3] Compare the Problems, XI. 14, ἡ δὲ φωνὴ κίνησίς ἐστι, and 35, ἡ φωνή ἐστιν ἀέρος κίνησις.

[4] K. von Jan claims it for Heraclides Ponticus (Mus. Scr. Gr., p. 51).

τὸν ἐχόμενον αὐτοῦ προωθῶν ὁμοίως, ὥστε πάντῃ τὴν φωνὴν διατείνειν τὴν αὐτήν, ἐφ᾽ ὅσον συμβαίνει γίγνεσθαι καὶ τοῦ ἀέρος τὴν κίνησιν. The last sentence seems to imply an actual transference of the air itself. So do the words (p. 801 a, 24 Bekker) ὁ γὰρ ὠσθεὶς ὑπὸ τῆς πληγῆς ἀὴρ μέχρι μέν τινος φέρεται συνεχής. Compare too in the Aristotelian *Problems*, XI. 6 (p. 61 v. Jan), ὁ ἀὴρ ὁ φερόμενος ποιεῖ τὸν ψόφον, (p. 63) ὁ δὲ ψόφος ἀήρ ἐστιν ὠθούμενος ὑπὸ ἀέρος, and XIX. 35 (p. 96) ἡ δὲ φωνὴ ἢ ἀέρος ἢ ἄλλου τινὸς φορά.

The view that sound is a formation of the air (τῷ τὸν ἀέρα σχηματίζεσθαι, καθάπερ οἴονταί τινες) appears in the *Problems* in the section περὶ φωνῆς.

XI. 23: διὰ τί, εἴπερ ἡ φωνή ἐστιν ἀήρ τις ἐσχηματισμένος καὶ φερόμενος, διαλύεται πολλάκις τὸ σχῆμα, ἡ δὲ ἠχὼ κτέ.

XI. 51: διὰ τί, εἴπερ ἡ φωνὴ ἀήρ τις ἐσχηματισμένος ἐστί, φερομένη διαλύεται πολλάκις τὸ σχῆμα, ἡ δὲ ἠχώ, ἣ γίνεται πληγέντος τοῦ τοιούτου πρός τι στερεόν, οὐ διαλύεται, ἀλλὰ σαφῶς ἀκούομεν ;

The distinction between defining sound as a blow on air and as air under the influence of a blow seems to have given trouble.

Aristides Quintilianus, *de musica*, p. 7,7 Meib.: ὕλη δὲ μουσικῆς φωνὴ καὶ κίνησις σώματος. τὴν δὲ φωνὴν οἱ μὲν ἀέρα πεπληγμένον, οἱ δέ, ἀέρος πληγὴν ἔφασαν, οἱ μέν, αὐτὸ τὸ σῶμα τὸ πεπονθὸς ἦχον, οἱ δ᾽, ὅπερ ἄμεινον, τὸ τούτου πάθος ὁρισάμενοι.

Aristotle, *Problems*, XI. 29: ὁ δὲ ψόφος ἀὴρ ἢ πάθος ἀέρος ἐστίν.

Ptolemy, *Harmonics*, I. i., p. 1 Wallis: ψόφος δὲ πάθος ἀκουστῶν.

See too Bryennius, I. sect. iv., p. 377 Wallis.

The following definitions are interesting :

Plutarch, *conviviales disputationes*, VIII. iii., p. 975: ἡ δὲ φωνὴ πληγὴ σώματος διηχοῦς· διηχὲς δὲ τὸ συμπαθὲς αὐτῷ καὶ συμφυές, εὐκίνητον δὲ καὶ κοῦφον καὶ ὁμαλὸν καὶ ὑπήκοον τοῦ δι᾽ εὐτονίαν καὶ συνέχειαν οἷός ἐστι παρ᾽ ἡμῖν ὁ ἀήρ.

Id. de placitis philosophorum, IV. xix., περὶ φωνῆς, 902 B, sq.: Πλάτων τὴν φωνὴν ὁρίζεται, πνεῦμα διὰ στόματος ἀπὸ διανοίας ἡγμένον, καὶ πληγὴν ὑπὸ ἀέρος δι' ὤτων καὶ ἐγκεφάλου καὶ αἵματος μέχρι ψυχῆς διαδιδομένην. Ἐπίκουρος, τὴν φωνὴν εἶναι ῥεῦμα ἐκπεμπόμενον ἀπὸ τῶν φωνούντων, ἢ ἠχούντων, ἢ ψοφούντων· τοῦτο δὲ τὸ ῥεῦμα εἰς ὁμοιοσχήμονα θρύπτεσθαι θραύσματα. Δημόκριτος, καὶ τὸν ἀέρα φησὶν εἰς ὁμοιοσχήμονα θρύπτεσθαι σώματα .... καὶ συνκαλινδεῖσθαι τοῖς ἐκ τῆς φωνῆς θραύσμασι.

Ibid., xx., εἰ ἀσώματος ἡ φωνή, καὶ πῶς ἠχὼ γίνεται, 902 F, sq.: Πυθαγόρας, Πλάτων, Ἀριστοτέλης ἀσώματον· οὐ γὰρ τὸν ἀέρα ἀλλὰ τὸ σχῆμα τὸ περὶ τὸν ἀέρα καὶ τὴν ἐπιφάνειαν κατὰ ποιὰν πλῆξιν γίνεσθαι φωνήν. πᾶσα δὲ ἐπιφάνεια ἀσώματος. .... οἱ δὲ Στωϊκοί, σῶμα τὴν φωνήν.

Ptolemy, Harm., I. iii., p. 6 Wallis: τάσις γάρ τίς ἐστι συνεχὴς τοῦ ἀέρος, ὁ ψόφος, ἀπὸ τοῦ τοῖς τὰς πληγὰς ποιοῦσιν ἐμπεριλαμβανομένου διήκουσα πρὸς τὸν ἐκτός.

Ibid., i., p. 1 : ψόφος δὲ πάθος ἀκουστῶν.

See too Bryennius, I. sect. iv., p. 377 Wallis.

We have already noticed (p. 3) that musical sounds may differ from one another in a number of ways. Before passing on to consider the definitions of the musical sound, it will not be out of place to dwell a moment on the classification of sounds in general.

One of the most evident principles in accordance with which sounds may be classified is that which distinguishes articulate and inarticulate sounds.

Aristotle defines articulate sound (φωνή) in the following passages :

Aristotle, de anima, II 8, 9, p. 420 b (p. 6 K. v. Jan): περὶ μὲν οὖν ψόφου ταύτῃ διωρίσθω· ἡ δὲ φωνὴ ψόφος τίς ἐστιν ἐμψύχου· τῶν γὰρ ἀψύχων οὐθὲν φωνεῖ, ἀλλὰ καθ' ὁμοιότητα λέγεται φωνεῖν, οἷον αὐλὸς καὶ λύρα καὶ ὅσα ἄλλα τῶν ἀψύχων ἀπότασιν[1] ἔχει καὶ μέλος καὶ διάλεκτον.

---

[1] ἀπότασιν. K. v. Jan, Mus. Scr. Gr., p. 6, explains: probabile est ἀπότασιν tanquam genus complecti ἐπίτασιν et ἄνεσιν. See below, p. 16.

Ibid., 11 (p. 7 K. v. Jan): ὥστε ἡ πληγὴ τοῦ ἀναπνεομένου ἀέρος ὑπὸ τῆς ἐν τούτοις τοῖς μορίοις ψυχῆς πρὸς τὴν καλουμένην ἀρτηρίαν φωνή ἐστιν· οὐ γὰρ πᾶς ζῴου ψόφος φωνή, καθάπερ εἴπομεν (ἔστι γὰρ καὶ τῇ γλώττῃ ψοφεῖν καὶ ὡς οἱ βήττοντες), ἀλλὰ δεῖ ἔμψυχόν τε εἶναι καὶ μετὰ φαντασίας τινός· σημαντικὸς γὰρ δή τις ψόφος ἐστὶν ἡ φωνὴ καὶ οὐ τοῦ ἀναπνεομένου ἀέρος ὥσπερ ὁ βήξ.

It appears, then, that whereas φωνή is used properly of the voice only, the term was applied also to the tones of musical instruments. Aristoxenus speaks of φωνὴ ὀργανική τε καὶ ἀνθρωπική (*Harm.*, p. 14 Meib.).

The analysis of articulate sound into its phonetic elements is important to the art of writing, and consequently the various vowel-sounds and consonant-sounds must have been differentiated from very early times, since it was this that led to the invention of writing by letters to take the place of ideographic writing.

Another important principle of division is involved in the distinction between musical and unmusical sounds. This classification concerns chiefly the Science of Music. As Phonetics disregards all but articulate sounds, so the Science of Music deals only with musical sounds. It should be observed that the line which separates musical sounds from unmusical sounds crosses that which separates articulate and inarticulate sounds. An articulate sound may be either musical or unmusical ; so may an inarticulate sound.

What, then, is meant by musical and unmusical or nonmusical? In the first place, the term 'musical,' as used in this connection, does not, of course, mean merely 'used in music.' In that case it would only be necessary to enumerate the kinds of sounds so used. On the contrary, many sounds which must be classed with musical sounds are unsuitable for use in music on account of difficulties attending their production or for some other reason ; and many unmusical sounds are used in music to produce certain effects, generally of a rhythmical nature. Nevertheless, it is true in a general way that those sounds which fall under the definition of musical sounds form the bulk of the sounds which music employs.

There is no difficulty in grasping the general notion on which the difference between musical and unmusical sounds rests. Everyone feels the difference which exists between the speaking voice and the singing voice, between the sound of a boatman's siren and the notes of a flute. In most cases it is easy to assign a sound to one or the other of these classes. It will sometimes, however, be difficult to decide in the case of certain complicated sounds whether they have more the character of musical notes or of noises. It then becomes necessary to make a rigorous definition of the musical sound, in order to ascertain on what basis the classification rests.

The definition of musical and unmusical sounds is usually made to depend on the steadiness or unsteadiness of the pitch of the sounds. For example, Mr. Sedley Taylor defines these sounds in the following words:[1] "A musical sound is one of *constant*, a non-musical sound one of *varying*, pitch."[2] But

---

[1] Sedley Taylor, *Sight Singing from the Established Notation* (Macmillan and Co., 1890), § 6.

[2] Compare too § 3, and the same author's *Sound and Music*, 2nd ed., § 23, p. 48: "The difference, then, between musical and non-musical sounds seems to lie in this, that the former are constant, while the latter are continually varying. The human voice can produce sounds of both classes. In singing a sustained note, it remains quite steady, neither rising nor falling. Its conversational tone, on the other hand, is perpetually varying in height even within a single syllable; directly it ceases so to vary, its non-musical character disappears, and it becomes what is commonly called 'sing-song.'"

Encyclopædia Britannica, I. p. 107 b, Art. *Acoustics* (David Thomson): "Besides the three qualities above mentioned [loudness, pitch, and timbre], there exists another point in which sounds may be distinguished among each other, and which, though perhaps reducible to difference of timbre, requires some special remarks, viz., that by which sounds are characterized, either as *noises* or as *musical notes*. A musical note is the result of regular periodic vibrations of the air-particles acting on the ear, and therefore also of the body whence they proceed, each particle passing through the same phase at stated intervals of time. On the other hand, the motion

this, the usual definition, is open to criticism in the following particulars. In the first place, it excludes from the category of musical sounds that union or binding of two notes known as portamento, which the violin class of instruments and the voice are capable of producing; for portamento must evidently be defined as a gradual change of pitch between fixed limits. In the second place, it admits such sounds as the tones of badly made bells, in which the pitch, such as it is, *may* remain constant and steady, but which it is best to class with non-musical sounds. Lastly, before the steadiness or the unsteadiness of the pitch of a sound is made the basis for a classification, would it not be better to select the actual presence or absence of pitch in the composition of the sound? To be sure, this would not enable us to draw a hard and fast line, owing to the fact that pitch may be present in varying quantities, but at least we could separate those sounds in which it is impossible to recognize any trace of pitch from those in which it is present to some extent, those sounds which are purely noisy from those which are to a certain extent musical. After that the steadiness or unsteadiness of the pitch could be used in making a subdivision of pitch-sounds, in which the sub-class of sounds of steady pitch would correspond to the class of musical sounds as commonly defined.

But there still remains the twofold objection that the peculiar variation in pitch above mentioned (portamento) is classed with 'non-musical' sounds, although it is distinctly musical, and that such sounds as the tones of badly cast bells, whose pitch is occasionally steady, are classed with musical sounds, although they are essentially noisy.

---

to which *noise* is due is irregular and flitting, alternately fast and slow, and creating in the mind a bewildering and confusing effect of a more or less unpleasant character. Noise may also be produced by combining in an arbitrary manner several musical notes, as when one leans with the forearm against the keys of a piano. In fact, the composition of regular periodic motions, thus effected, is equivalent to an irregular motion."

In the last division (that in which sounds of constant pitch were separated from sounds of varying pitch) the principle employed was the behavior of pitch from moment to moment, its changeability or constancy. We are now led to suggest another principle which might be used to subdivide once again those sounds which are characterized by the presence of pitch. It is the complexity or simplicity of the arrangement of the various heights or degrees of pitch which are present at any and every point of time in every sound except the theoretically pure tone of science. If the constituent pitches are arranged with reference to some principle of order, so that the pitches are related, the sound will be musical, and on this order will depend the quality or timbre of the note. On the other hand, if the arrangement is disorderly, the sound will be unmusical or noisy. As we have noticed before, a bell may have been so unsuccessfully cast that, apart from the variation so noticeable from time to time, the different parts give forth sounds of different and unrelated pitches. The result is a noise. If all the keys of a piano which one can cover with the hand are sounded at once, a noise is produced.

Applying this principle of order in the constituent pitches to the class of sounds whose pitch is constant, we obtain two sections, into one of which all sounds which it seems inappropriate to call 'musical' will be collected. Similarly, in the coördinate class of sounds whose pitch varies, one section will comprise those sounds which are musical in every particular except the variation in pitch (e. g., the glide of the portamento, the sound of a boatman's siren), the other will include sounds which are noisy both from the quality of the tone and from the variation in the pitch (e. g., the creaking of a hinge).

If we use this principle of order in a slightly different manner, we may subdivide varying sounds according as the variation is orderly and limited by fixed bounds (e. g., portamento), or is not. When orderly, the variation is generally in the control of the artist (violinist or singer). Disorderly variation is the characteristic of sounds like the howling of the wind.[1]

We have seen that every musical sound is characterized by the presence of pitch, and that the behavior of pitch is used as the basis for the separation of musical sounds from unmusical sounds. Before proceeding to discuss the ancient definitions of the musical sound and to compare the ancient classifications with those employed in modern works, a few words must be said in regard to pitch itself and to the manner in which it is handled in the Greek treatises.

Pitch is that sensation in which the differences are expressed by the terms acute and grave, high and low, shrill and deep, sharp and flat. Physically pitch may be defined as regularity in the vibrations of air, and the degree of pitch depends on the rapidity or frequency of the vibrations, or on the length of

---

[1] CLASSIFICATION OF SOUNDS.

A. characterized by the presence of pitch (pitch-sounds).

    a. those in which the pitch is *constant* ('musical').

        α. orderly disposition of constituent pitches. MUSICAL.

        β. disorderly disposition of constituent pitches. NOISY.

    b. those in which the pitch is *varying* ('non-musical').

        α. (as above) sometimes musical.

        β. (as above) always noisy.

or

        1. orderly variation of pitch. MUSICAL.

        2. disorderly variation of pitch. UNMUSICAL.

B. characterized by the absence of pitch.

their period. Inasmuch as, if we omit from consideration the element of duration in time, sounds differ from one another in three most prominent particulars,[1] their loudness (force, intensity), their timbre (quality, *Klang-Farbe*), and their pitch, any one of these qualities or properties may be described as that particular in which a sound varies, if the other two are kept constant. If, then, the notes of one and the same instrument are sounded with the same degree of loudness, the notes will differ only in their pitch. Although Helmholtz's discovery that ordinary musical notes are composed of a number of related pitches, of which one is predominent, is now universally accepted, and although timbre is thus reduced to a matter of pitches, the threefold division of the character of musical sounds is still useful. By the pitch of a note, then, the predominant pitch is generally meant, and since there is no indication that timbre was analyzed in this way by any of the ancients, we shall not have to do with any but this, the nominal pitch of a musical sound.

But it is by no means certain that the existence of the vibrations by which sound is produced was unknown to the Greeks. The passage from the Aristotelian *de audibilibus*, quoted at p. 7, seems to show that the nature of the motion of the air was suspected, if not proved. Still more suggestive are the last words of the following passage:

Aristotle, *de anima*, II 8, 7 (p. 5 K. v. Jan): ἔστι γὰρ ὁ ψόφος κίνησις τοῦ δυναμένου κινεῖσθαι τὸν τρόπον τοῦτον ὅνπερ τὰ ἀφαλλόμενα ἀπὸ τῶν λείων, ὅταν τις κρούσῃ. οὐ δὴ πᾶν ὥσπερ εἴρηται ψοφεῖ τυπτόμενον καὶ τύπτον, οἷον ἐὰν πατάξῃ βελόνη βελόνην· ἀλλὰ δεῖ τὸ τυπτόμενον ὁμαλὸν εἶναι, ὥστε τὸν ἀέρα ἀθροῦν ἀφάλλεσθαι καὶ σείεσθαι.

Furthermore we have Aristotle, *Problems*, XIX. 39 : ἡ δευτέρα τῆς νεάτης πληγὴ τοῦ ἀέρος ὑπάτη ἐστίν, and the prac-

---

[1]*Encyclopædia Britannica*, I. p. 107 b: "Sounds in general exhibit three different qualities, so far as their effect on the ear is concerned, viz., *loudness, pitch,* and *timbre.*"

tice of certain writers of assigning the greater number in a ratio to the higher note. K. von Jan distinctly claims a knowledge of the vibrations of the air for the ancients.[1] The Greek words for pitch, τάσις and τόνος, are of course connected with the idea of stretching. It would be observed from stringed instruments that increase in the tension produced a heightening of the pitch (ἐπίτασις), and that relaxation produced a lowering (ἄνεσις). Height of pitch or high pitch is expressed by ὀξύτης, the reverse by βαρύτης; ὀξύς and βαρύς are the words for acute and grave.

A rigorous definition of pitch does not seem to have been attempted in the ancient works on musical science. It was usual to define the term either by means of ὀξύτης and βαρύτης, or by means of ἐπίτασις and ἄνεσις. In the former method the idea of height and depth in pitch was assumed and pitch itself was defined as that which is common to these. This is the course pursued by Claudius Ptolemy, the Alexandrian mathematician, astronomer, and geographer.

Ptolemy, *Harmonics*, I. iv., p. 8 Wallis: ὁ γὰρ οὕτω λεγόμενος τόνος κοινὸν ἂν εἴη γένος τῆς ὀξύτητος καὶ τῆς βαρύτητος, παρ' ἓν εἶδος τὸ τῆς τάσεως εἰλημμένος, ὡς τὸ πέρας τοῦ τέλους καὶ τῆς ἀρχῆς. As 'limit' covers both 'end' and 'beginning,' so τόνος both ὀξύτης and βαρύτης.[2]

In the other method of defining pitch, the changes in pitch observed in the tones of the human voice and in those of musical instruments produced the concept of an upward and downward motion, and pitch was defined as the absence of such motion, that is, as standing or rest. This is the method employed by Aristoxenus. Τάσις is defined as μονή τις καὶ στάσις τῆς φωνῆς (*Harmonics*, I. § 31, p. 12 Meib.), or as ἠρεμία φωνῆς (*Ibid.* I. § 32, p. 13 Meib.: ἡ δὲ τάσις ὅτι μὲν οὔτ' ἐπίτασις οὔτ' ἄνεσίς ἐστι παντελῶς δῆλον,—τὴν μὲν γὰρ

---

[1] K. von Jan, *Musici Scriptores Graeci*, p. 135.

[2] Compare Porphyry, *commentarius*, p. 258 Wallis: ἔστι γὰρ καὶ ἡ βαρύτης τάσις καὶ ἡ ὀξύτης τάσις.

εἶναί φαμεν ἠρεμίαν φωνῆς, τὰς δ' ἐν τοῖς ἔμπροσθεν εὕρομεν
οὔσας κινήσεις τινάς). Conversely στάσις (or ἑστάναι) is
defined by the help of τάσις: δεῖ δὲ καταμανθάνειν ὅτι τὸ μὲν
ἑστάναι τὴν φωνὴν τὸ μένειν ἐπὶ μιᾶς τάσεώς ἐστι (§ 32, p. 13
Meib.). Of course, strictly speaking, what is defined in this
definition of τάσις is not so much 'pitch' as 'degree of pitch.'

It is now necessary to compare some of the ancient classifications of sounds with those of modern theory, and so to
discuss the φθόγγος or 'musical sound,' the unit of the science
of music.

Aristoxenus set the example for a number of followers by
leading up to the definition of the musical sound through a
careful analysis of what is termed κίνησις φωνῆς, the motion
of the voice.[1] He says that a description of the various kinds
of κίνησις is necessary for the proper definition of the φθόγγος.[2]
In this description it will not be difficult to see what sort of
a classification of sounds Aristoxenus must be understood to
have had in mind.

It is evident that the passage from one degree of pitch to
another must be made in one of two ways. Either the pitch
of a sound changes suddenly from the initial state to the final
state, in such a way that at no moment does the sound rest
at, or pass through, any intermediate degree of pitch ; or the
pitch changes gradually in the direction of the final degree
of pitch, that is, either upward or downward, and so passes
through every possible intermediate degree, but rests at none.
These are the only two ways in which a sound emanating
from one and the same instrument can pass from one pitch to
another. They may be compared to stepping and gliding.
In the one case the intermediate space is leapt over, in the
other it is traversed.

---

[1] Φωνή is here used of the tones of musical instruments in general, not of
the voice alone. See above, pp. 9, 10.
[2] Aristoxenus, Harmonics, I. § 4, p. 3 Meib.: καί τοι τούτου μὴ διορισθέντος
οὐ πάνυ ῥᾴδιον εἰπεῖν περὶ φθόγγου τί ποτ' ἐστίν.

2

If now we consider the flow of sound proceeding from any instrument and regard only the manner in which change of pitch takes place, it is plain that the former of the two manners mentioned above (sudden changes) implies for practical purposes rest at various stages, that is to say, there will be a period of fixed pitch before and after each leap.[1] The second manner (gradual changes) implies nothing as to periods of fixed or stationary pitch. The glides may connect what are called notes or musical sounds,[2] or there may be no such notes, the pitch may never become fixed, but may wander up and down at random. But when the pitch does remain fixed before and after a glide, we have the phenomenon of portamento (see above, p. 12), in which the two manners combine.

Returning to Aristoxenus, we find that κίνησις φωνῆς (briefly, change of pitch) is divided into two kinds of movement, κίνησις συνεχής and κίνησις διαστηματική.[3] Of these the former, *continuous* movement, is that in which *not only* are the changes in pitch continuous, *but* there are no periods of fixed pitch. The latter, *discrete* movement (intervallate) is that in which the pitch leaps over intervals and then rests at various degrees of pitch.

The passage in which this subject is dealt with runs as follows:

Aristoxenus, *Harm.*, I. § 26, p. 8 Meib.: κατὰ μὲν οὖν τὴν συνεχῆ, τόπον τινὰ διεξιέναι φαίνεται ἡ φωνὴ τῇ αἰσθήσει, οὕτως ὡς ἂν μηδαμοῦ ἱσταμένη < ἢ >, μηδ᾽ ἐπ᾽ αὐτῶν τῶν περάτων, κατά γε τὴν τῆς αἰσθήσεως φαντασίαν, ἀλλὰ φερομένη συνεχῶς μέχρι σιωπῆς. κατὰ δὲ τὴν ἑτέραν, ἣν ὀνομάζομεν διαστηματικήν, ἐναντίως φαίνεται κινεῖσθαι· διαβαίνουσα

---

[1] We can, of course, conceive of a glide taking place immediately after a step, but such a performance may safely be omitted from consideration.

[2] See above, p. 11.

[3] Aristoxenus, *Harmonics*, I. § 25, p. 8 Meib.: πάσης δὲ φωνῆς δυναμένης κινεῖσθαι τὸν εἰρημένον αὐτὸν τρόπον, δύο τινές εἰσιν ἰδέαι κινήσεως, ἥ τε συνεχὴς καὶ ἡ διαστηματική.

γὰρ ἵστησιν αὐτὴν ἐπὶ μιᾶς τάσεως, εἶτα πάλιν ἐφ᾽ ἑτέρας, καὶ
τοῦτο ποιοῦσα συνεχῶς—λέγω δὲ συνεχῶς κατὰ τὸν χρόνον—
ὑπερβαίνουσα μὲν τοὺς περιεχομένους ὑπὸ τῶν τάσεων τόπους,
ἱσταμένη δ᾽ ἐπ᾽ αὐτῶν τῶν τάσεων, καὶ φθεγγομένη ταύτας
μόνον αὐτὰς μελῳδεῖν λέγεται, καὶ κινεῖσθαι διαστηματικὴν
κίνησιν. And further on, *Ibid.*, § 27, p. 9, 11 Meib. : ἁπλῶς
γὰρ ὅταν οὕτω κινῆται ἡ φωνή, ὥστε μηδαμοῦ δοκεῖν ἵστασθαι
τῇ ἀκοῇ, συνεχῆ λέγομεν ταύτην τὴν κίνησιν· ὅταν δὲ στῆναί
που δόξασα, εἶτα πάλιν διαβαίνειν τινὰ τόπον φανῇ, καὶ τοῦτο
ποιήσασα, πάλιν ἐφ᾽ ἑτέρας τάσεως στῆναι δόξῃ, καὶ τοῦτο
ἐναλλὰξ ποιεῖν φαινομένη συνεχῶς διατελῇ, διαστηματικὴν
τὴν τοιαύτην κίνησιν λέγομεν.[1]

Aristoxenus next identifies these two kinds of voice-move-
ment with the singing and the speaking voice.

Aristoxenus, *Harm.*, I. § 28, p. 9, 20 Meib.: τὴν μὲν οὖν
συνεχῆ, λογικὴν εἶναί φαμεν. διαλεγομένων γὰρ ἡμῶν, οὕτως
ἡ φωνὴ κινεῖται κατὰ τόπον, ὥστε μηδαμοῦ δοκεῖν ἵστασθαι.
κατά γε τὴν ἑτέραν, ἣν ὀνομάζομεν διαστηματικήν, ἐναντίως
πέφυκε γίγνεσθαι. ἀλλὰ γὰρ ἵστασθαί τε δοκεῖ, καὶ πάντες
τὸν τοῦτο φαινόμενον ποιεῖν οὐκέτι λέγειν φασίν, ἀλλ᾽ ἄδειν·
διόπερ ἐν τῷ διαλέγεσθαι φεύγομεν τὸ ἑστάναι (ἱστάναι libb.)
τὴν φωνήν,[2] ἂν μὴ διὰ πάθος ποτὲ εἰς τοιαύτην κίνησιν ἀναγ-
κασθῶμεν ἐλθεῖν· ἐν δὲ τῷ μελῳδεῖν τοὐτάντιον ποιοῦμεν.
τὸ μὲν γὰρ συνεχὲς φεύγομεν, τὸ δὲ ἑστάναι τὴν φωνὴν ὡς
μάλιστα διώκομεν· ὅσῳ γὰρ μᾶλλον ἑκάστην τῶν φωνῶν μίαν
τε καὶ ἑστηκυίαν καὶ τὴν αὐτὴν ποιήσομεν, τοσούτῳ φαίνεται τῇ αἰσθήσει τὸ μέλος ἀκριβέστερον. ὅτι μὲν δύο κινήσεων
οὐσῶν κατὰ τόπον τῆς φωνῆς, ἡ μὲν συνεχὴς λογική τίς ἐστιν,
ἡ δὲ διαστηματικὴ μελῳδική, σχεδὸν δῆλον ἐκ τῶν εἰρημένων.

Here then lies the justification for attaching importance to
the motion of the voice and for analyzing it in the way which
Aristoxenus does. The Greeks were very sensitive to the
changes in pitch which accompany the spoken sentence. We

---

[1] Cf. Bryennius, III. p. 375 Wallis. 　　　　[2] Compare p. 11².

have only to point to the fact that their written accents express this rise and fall in pitch. It was natural then that a comparison should be instituted between the formal melody of vocal music and that more subtle melody which exists in conversational speech. It is also important to remember that the voice held a predominant position in Greek music, possibly due quite as much to the inferiority of the musical instruments of the ancients as to any greater appreciation of the capabilities of the voice on their part.

Aristoxenus is now ready to describe the φθόγγος (musical sound), having prepared the way for it by his discussion of the two sorts of κίνησις. He says (*Harm.*, I. § 31, p. 12 Meib.): κινεῖται μὲν γὰρ (ἡ φωνὴ) ἐν τῷ διάστημά τι ποιεῖν, ἵσταται δ᾽ ἐν τῷ φθόγγῳ. The stopping places of κίνησις διαστηματική are φθόγγοι. At p. 15 Meib. there is a different definition (see below, p. 27).

We have noticed (p. 18) that the 'continuous movement' of the voice, as described by Aristoxenus, does not include a gradual change of pitch, if bounded by fixed degrees of pitch. The treatment may be said to be faulty to that extent. In fact, the difference between the two kinds of motion, when analyzed, turns out to be more a difference of steadiness and unsteadiness in pitch than simply a difference in the manner in which it may change from acute to grave and *vice versá*. In κίνησις συνεχής the pitch is nowhere steady and is always varying; in κίνησις διαστηματική it is steady now at this height, now at that, and never varies except by leaps. The sounds which constitute the former are then to be found in the class of sounds commonly styled 'non-musical,' those which constitute the latter, in the 'musical' class.[1]

Although no provision is made for gradual change in pitch bounded by fixed degrees of pitch—in a word, for portamento—

---

[1] The classes *A b* and *A a*, respectively, in the classification given at p. 14, note. The subdivisions β are, of course, to be omitted.

21

in the Aristoxenean treatment of pitch changes,[1] this form of movement (which may be described as a continuous movement modified by the periods of rest characteristic of discrete movement) was not overlooked, but was noticed only to be passed over. Aristoxenus, *Harm.*, I. § 27, p. 9 Meib. : ληπτέον δὲ ἑκάτερον τούτων (the two forms of motion) κατὰ τὴν αἰσθήσεως φαντασίαν. πότερον μὲν γὰρ δύνατον ἢ ἀδύνατον φωνὴν κινεῖσθαι καὶ (ἡ Meib.) πάλιν ἵστασθαι αὐτὴν ἐπὶ μιᾶς τάσεως, ἑτέρας ἐστὶ σκέψεως, καὶ πρὸς τὴν ἐνεστῶσαν πραγματείαν οὐκ ἀναγκαῖον, τὸ διακινῆσαι (δὲ κινῆσαι libb.) τούτων ἑκάτερον. ὁποτέρως γὰρ ἔχει τὸ αὐτὸ ποιεῖ πρός γε τὸ χωρίσαι τὴν ἐμμελῆ κίνησιν τῆς φωνῆς ἀπὸ τῶν ἄλλων κινήσεων.

But it is not easy to see why continuous motion as a whole should not be omitted, if that modification of it which admits periods of rest at fixed pitches is rejected, inasmuch as the latter is far more musical in its nature than the former. Without steadiness in the pitch it would be almost impossible to gain an idea of musical interval, and all music is based on interval, or the relation which subsists between musical notes. Mr. Hubert Parry says:[2] "Just as among the early ancestors of our species, speech would begin when the indefinite noises which they first used to communicate with one another, like animals, passed into some definite sound which conveyed to the savage ear some definite and constant meaning; so the indefinite cries and shouts which expressed their feelings began to pass into music when a few definite notes were made to take the place of vague irregular shouting." And again, a little further on : "So the resources of music increased as the relations of more and more definite notes were established, in obedience to the development of musical instinct, and as

[1] *A b*, 1 in the classification on p. 14.
[2] C. Hubert H. Parry, *The Art of Music*, p. 6.

the ear learnt to appreciate the intervals and the mind to retain the simple fragments of tune which resulted." The Aristoxenean κίνησις συνεχής (fixed pitch entirely absent) would thus seem to characterize the earliest attempts at music, whereas the κίνησις διαστηματική is peculiar to fully organized music. It would even appear from the last part of the passage quoted at p. 19 (ἐν δὲ τῷ μελῳδεῖν, etc.) that portamento was avoided as much as possible by the Greeks in singing, although it is likely that this phenomenon represents an intermediate stage in the development of music. We quote again from Mr. Parry's work on the *Art of Music*.[1] "At the very bottom of the process of development are those savage howls which have hardly any distinct notes in them at all. Many travellers record such things, and try to represent them in the European musical stave. For instance, the natives of Australia are described by a French traveller as beginning a howl on a high note and descending a full octave in semitones." But the author shows that this cannot be an accurate description of the process, "as a downward scale of correct semitones is beyond the powers of any but very highly trained singers." "In all such cases the process must have been a gliding of the voice up or down, without notes that were strictly defined either in relation to one another or to any general principle."

Musical notes must evidently have first made their appearance when the bounds of such glides assumed a fixed nature and relationship with each other. The statement in Helmholtz[2] that "The first fact that we meet with in the music of all nations, so far as is yet known, is that alterations of pitch in melodies take place by intervals, and not by continuous transitions," is at variance with the above. It seems to overlook the fact that we can describe an interval equally well by gliding through the space as by leaping over it.

---

[1] *Op. cit.*, p. 53.
[2] Helmholtz, *Sensations of Tone*, 2nd English Ed. (1885), by Alexander J. Ellis, p. 250.

23

Aristides Quintilianus not only recognizes the existence of portamento, but provides a place for it in his threefold division of κίνησις φωνῆς. Aristides Quintilianus, de musica, p. 7 Meib.: ἡ δὲ δὴ κίνησις ὑφέστηκεν ἐν διαφόροις χρόνοις. χρόνος γάρ ἐστι μέτρον κινήσεως καὶ στάσεως. τῆς δὲ κινήσεως ἡ μὲν ἁπλῆ πέφυκεν, ἡ δὲ οὐχ ἁπλῆ. καὶ ταύτης ἡ μὲν συνεχής, ἡ δὲ διαστηματική, ἡ δὲ μέση. συνεχὴς μὲν οὖν ἐστι φωνὴ ἡ τάς τε ἀνέσεις καὶ τὰς ἐπιτάσεις λεληθότως διά τι τάχος ποιουμένη. διαστηματικὴ δὲ ἡ τὰς μὲν τάσεις φανερὰς ἔχουσα, τὰ δὲ τούτων μέτρα λεληθότα. μέση δὲ ἡ ἐξ ἀμφοῖν συγκειμένη. ἡ μὲν οὖν συνεχής ἐστιν ᾗ διαλεγόμεθα. μέση δὲ ᾗ τὰς τῶν ποιημάτων ἀναγνώσεις ποιούμεθα. διαστηματικὴ δὲ—ἡ καὶ τὰ μέσον τῶν ἁπλῶν ποσὰ ποιουμένη διαστήματα καὶ μονὰς— ἥτις καὶ μελῳδικὴ καλεῖται.[1]

We must now consider the method employed by the great Pythagorean (using the term in its musical application), Claudius Ptolemy. His *Harmonics* in three books is of equal importance with the musical works of Aristoxenus and Aristides Quintilianus. Ptolemy may be considered to be the representative of the more mathematical of the two great rival schools of musical theorists, the Aristoxeneans and the Pythagoreans. Aristides is classed by Gevaert as an eclectic.

In order to fix the position of musical sounds[2] in relation to other sounds, Ptolemy proceeds in his treatise in the following manner. After two preliminary chapters, he devotes a

---

[1] Aristides' Classification:

κίνησις ἁπλῆ.

κίνησις οὐχ ἁπλῆ { συνεχής. μέση. διαστηματική.

For the meaning of κίνησις ἁπλῆ, see pp. 27 and 29, 8. Κίνησις οὐχ ἁπλῆ seems to be the same as Aristoxenus' κίνησις φωνῆς in general.

[2] The word for sound in general, ψόφος, Wallis renders by *sonitus* in his Latin translation; the word for musical sound, φθόγγος, by *sonus*.

chapter to pitch, and then one to sounds[1] and their differences. The separation of sounds into two classes according as pitch is present or absent is implied (unless, to be sure, pitch is attributed to all sounds whatsoever). The first classification we meet with is that by which sounds which have a pitch are divided into two groups according to the nature of that pitch. Ψόφοι, he says (Ptolemy, *Harm.*, I. iv., p. 8 Wallis), are either ἰσότονοι or ἀνισότονοι; the former are sounds which are unchangeable in the matter of pitch (ἀπαράλλακτοι κατὰ τὸν τόνον), the latter are those which change their pitch (παραλλάσσοντες).[2]

Ptolemy next takes ψόφοι ἀνισότονοι and divides them into οἱ συνεχεῖς and οἱ διωρισμένοι.[3] Definitions follow. "Con-

---

[1] The title of the chapter, περὶ φθόγγων, καὶ τῶν ἐν αὐτοῖς διαφορῶν, must be wrong. Read περὶ ψόφων κτέ.

[2] The equality and inequality of pitch implied in the words ἰσότονος and ἀνισότονος refer, of course, in this passage to the possibility of change which any sound may undergo in the course of its existence. But these terms are also used in a very different sense—a sense which is met with in the next chapter of Ptolemy's treatise, and even at the end of the present chapter. Ambiguity in the use of terms has always been in Music a peculiarly fertile source of misunderstanding. The difference in the meanings is well stated by Porphyry in his commentary on this passage (*commentarius*, c. 4, p. 258 Wallis). The second use of the words will not cause any difficulty, since the difference is so clear. In this meaning the τόνος refers to the pitch of notes as *compared* with *other* notes, and used in this way the terms are of frequent service in demonstrations of the Pythagorean theory of consonances. Porphyry's words are: ῥητέον πάλιν, ὡς ἰσότονος ὁ ψόφος λέγεται διχῶς· ὁ μὲν ἄλλῳ ψόφῳ ἴσην τὴν τάσιν κεκτημένος, ὥσπερ ἡ νήτη συνημμένων τῇ παρανήτῃ διεζευγμένων λέγεται εἶναι ἰσότονος. (Similarly we might say that E sharp in the key of B Major was 'equitonic' with F, or C sharp with D flat.) Such an ἰσότονος ψόφος, Porphyry continues, is more properly called ὁμότονος, and not merely ψόφος, but φθόγγος. The other meaning refers to the parts of one and the same sound, as the beginning, middle, and end. Such a sound, he says, might with more exactness be called ὁμοιομερής.

[3] It may be well at this point to tabulate Ptolemy's classes of sounds:

$$\psi\acute{o}\phi o\iota \begin{cases} \mathrm{\iota\sigma\acute{o}\tau ovo\iota.} \\ \mathrm{\grave{a}v\iota\sigma\acute{o}\tau ovo\iota} \begin{cases} \mathrm{\sigma uve\chi e\hat{\iota}s.} \\ \mathrm{\delta\iota\omega\rho\iota\sigma\mu\acute{e}vo\iota} = \phi\theta\acute{o}\gamma\gamma o\iota. \end{cases} \end{cases}$$

tinuous sounds are those in which the regions (τόποι) of the changes (in pitch) in each direction are not manifest, or in which no part whatever is ἰσότονος for a perceptible interval (of time). The same sort of thing is seen in the case of the colors of the rainbow. Of such a nature are those sounds which sound at the same time as their pitch is being raised or lowered, even while this change is being produced." The lowing of cattle and the howling of wolves are given as examples of these continuous sounds. Porphyry[1] adds the attempts of the beginner at singing, who cannot strike the right pitch at first, but feels for it.[2] He also gives as an instance the tuning of stringed instruments. All such 'continuous' sounds are unfit for music.

Ptolemy's second class, 'discrete' sounds—ψόφοι (ἀνισότονοι) διωρισμένοι—he. defines as sounds " in which the regions of the changes (in pitch) are manifest." The spaces or pitch-distances traversed are measurable, or such sounds arise when their parts remain 'equitonic' for a perceptible interval of time. As a parallel he gives the juxtaposition of pure and unmixed colors. Sounds like these are suitable for music, because they are bounded by ἰσότονοι ψόφοι and may be measured by their excesses (ὑπεροχαί), that is, by their ratios.

Continuous sounds are, then, sounds in which the variation in pitch takes place in such a way that it advances by insensible gradations and that it has no defined limits. Discrete sounds are those in which the pitch moves over well-defined distances. The two classes are characterized precisely by the two kinds of κίνησις explained by Aristoxenus—the continu-

---

[1] See K. v. Jan, *Mus. Scr. Gr.*, p. 116, on the authorship of the *commentarius in Ptolemaei harmonica.*

[2] Porphyry, comm., p. 260 Wallis: ζητεῖ πάντα τὸν σύνεγγυς τόπον τῆς ἐκδοθείσης τάσεως· καὶ βαρυτέρας μὲν τῆς ἰδίας προφορᾶς αἴσθησιν λαβών, παροξύνει κατ' ὀλίγον, αἰσθητὸν διάστημα μηδὲν ποιῶν· ὀξυτέρας δέ, βαρύνει πάλιν πρὸς ὀλίγον· ταῦτα δὲ ποιῶν συνεχῆ μὲν τὴν τάσιν τῆς φωνῆς ποιεῖ, ἐπὶ μίαν δὲ καὶ ὁμοίαν καὶ ἴσην τάσιν οὐκέτι, οὐδὲ ἰσοτόνως.

3

ous and the discrete or intervallate. And just as these two motions are appropriate to speech and song respectively, so ψόφοι συνεχεῖς, having no unity (Ptol., *Harm.*, I. iv., p. 8 Wallis: μηδαμῆ μηθὲν ὑποβάλλοντες ἐν καὶ ταὐτό), are unsuitable for music, while ψόφοι διωρισμένοι are suitable, and are now, after the definitions have been completed, called by Ptolemy φθόγγοι (*ibid.*, p. 9: καὶ δὴ φθόγγους ἤδη καλοῖμεν ἂν τοὺς τοιούτους, ὅτι φθόγγος ἐστὶ ψόφος ἕνα καὶ τὸν αὐτὸν ἐπέχων τόνον).

But if discrete sounds are φθόγγοι and keep the same pitch, why are they classed by Ptolemy with ψόφοι ἀνισότονοι rather than with ἰσότονοι? It is evident that discrete sounds may be analyzed into a series of ἰσότονοι. They are ἀνισότονοι only with reference to one another; each regarded by itself is ἰσότονος. It would seem that Ptolemy had in mind large masses or groups of sounds. As an example of ψόφοι ἰσότονοι he might have given the tones of such instruments as can produce only one note, like certain whistles and horns or the cymbals. The difficulty arises from attempting to regard as a unit too great a body of sound, too long a period of time. It is best to analyze such sounds as the tones of a flute into a series of separate sounds. This Ptolemy does not seem to have done. Wishing to include in his classification his ψόφοι ἀνισότονοι συνεχεῖς, and being unable to choose a simple unit from the mass of wavering sound, he seems to have been led to include among the ἀνισότονοι sounds which differed from the above as singing differs from speaking. In this way the old Aristoxenean treatment of κίνησις φωνῆς crops out.[1]

If now we compare Ptolemy's classification of sounds with Aristides' classification of the kinds of κίνησις φωνῆς (see the tables on pp. 23[1] and 24[3]), it will be observed that the same

---

[1] The two uses (see p. 24[8]) of the words ἰσότονος and ἀνισότονος are thus in danger of losing their distinction of meaning, if it is permitted to regard a number of sounds as one. In the term suggested by Porphyry, ὁμοιομερής (and ἀνομοιομερής, if used), the μέρη are better regarded as separate sounds.

scheme seems to have been followed (except for the presence in the latter of κίνησις μέση). Κίνησις ἁπλῆ thus appears as merely a time-progression and not a progression in pitch. The utterance is uniform, monotonous, whereas κίνησις οὐχ ἁπλῆ brings in the element of variation in pitch. In another respect the Ptolemaic classification of sounds is not quite rigorously logical. Like the Aristoxenean, it has no place for portamento sounds. These sounds, or rather the glide which joins the bounding notes, must be classed under ψόφοι ἀνισότονοι, but can find a place among neither the συνεχεῖς nor the διωρισμένοι.

Other definitions of the musical φθόγγος must now be quoted. Aristoxenus, we have seen (p. 20), defines φθόγγοι as the elements of his κίνησις διαστηματική. Another definition is found at p. 15 Meib.: φωνῆς πτῶσις ἐπὶ μίαν τάσιν, ὁ φθόγγος.

The definition of Thrasyllus we owe to Theon of Smyrna. Theo Smyrnaeus, de musica, c. 2, p. 47, sq. Hiller: Θράσυλλος τοίνυν περὶ τῆς ἐν ὀργάνῳ αἰσθητῆς λέγων ἁρμονίας, φθόγγον φησὶν εἶναι φωνῆς ἐναρμονίου τάσιν. ἐναρμόνιος δὲ λέγεται, ἐπὰν δύνηται καὶ τοῦ ὀξέος ὀξύτερος εὑρεθῆναι καὶ τοῦ βαρέος βαρύτερος· [καὶ ὁ αὐτὸς οὗτος καὶ μέσος ἐστίν.] ὡς εἴγε τινὰ τοιαύτην φωνὴν νοήσαιμεν ἥτις ὑπεραίρει πᾶσαν ὀξύτητα, οὐκ ἂν εἴη ἐναρμόνιος· οὐδὲ γὰρ τὸν τῆς ὑπερμεγέθους βροντῆς ψόφον ἐναρμόνιον ἐροῦμεν, ὅς γε καὶ ὀλέθριος διὰ τὴν ὑπερβολὴν πολλάκις γίνεται, ὥς τις ἔφη·

πολλοὺς δὲ βροντῆς τραῦμ' ἄναιμον ὤλεσε.

καὶ μὴν εἴ τις οὕτως βαρὺς εἴη φθόγγος, ὡς μὴ ἔχειν αὐτοῦ βαρύτερον, οὐκ ἂν οὐδὲ φθόγγος εἴη τὸ ἐναρμόνιον οὐκ ἔχων. διὰ τοῦτ' οὖν φθόγγος εἶναι λέγεται οὐ πᾶσα φωνὴ οὐδὲ πάσης φωνῆς τάσις, ἀλλ' ἡ ἐναρμόνιος, οἷον μέσης, νεάτης, ὑπάτης. Quoted verbatim, except ὅς γε καὶ .... ὤλεσε, by Bryennius.

The restriction imposed by the word ἐναρμόνιος confines the musical sound to the limits of the recognized scale.

Ptolemy, as we have seen (p. 26), defines φθόγγος in the words (*Harm.*, I. iv., p. 9 Wallis): φθόγγος ἐστὶ ψόφος ἕνα καὶ τὸν αὐτὸν ἐπέχων τόνον. Nicomachus, *harmonices manuale*, 4, p. 7 Meib. (p. 242 K. v. J.): καθόλου γάρ φαμεν ψόφον μὲν εἶναι πλῆξιν ἀέρος ἄθρυπτον μέχρι ἀκοῆς· φθόγγον δέ, φωνῆς ἐμμελοῦς ἁπλατῆ τάσιν· τάσιν δὲ μονήν τινα καὶ ταυτότητα κατὰ μέγεθος φθόγγου ἀδιαστάτου. *Ibid.*, 12, p. 24 Meib. (p. 261 K. v. J.): φθόγγος ἐστὶ φωνὴ ἄτομος οἷον μονὰς κατ' ἀκοήν· ὡς δὲ οἱ νεώτεροι, ἐπίπτωσις φωνῆς ἐπὶ μίαν τάσιν καὶ ἁπλῆν. ὡς δ' ἔνιοι, ἦχος ἁπλατὴς κατὰ τόπον ἀδιάστατος.

Porphyry, in his commentary on the above passage from Ptolemy's *Harmonics*, says that Ptolemy changed the usual definition of φθόγγος.

Porphyry, *comm. ad Ptol.*, c. iv., p. 262 Wallis: Εἶτα ἀποδίδωσιν ὅρον τοῦ φθόγγου, φθόγγος γάρ ἐστι ψόφος ἕνα καὶ τὸν αὐτὸν ἐπέχων τόνου, τόνον μὲν λαμβάνων ἀντὶ τῆς τάσεως καθάπερ ἤδη κέχρηται, τοὺς δὲ φερομένους ὅρους τοῦ φθόγγου μεταλαβών. φέρονται γὰρ αὐτοῦ ὅροι παρὰ μὲν τοῖς Πυθαγορείοις, φθόγγος ἐστὶ ψόφος παρὰ μίαν τάσιν ἐκφερόμενος, παρὰ δὲ τοῖς Ἀριστοξενίοις φθόγγος ἐστὶ φωνῆς ἐμμελοῦς πτῶσις ἐπὶ μίαν τάσιν, ἢ ἐμμελὴς φωνῆς πτῶσις ἐπὶ μίαν τάσιν. φωνῆς μὲν ἐμμελοῦς εἴρηται ἐπείπερ οὐ περὶ πάσης φωνῆς ὁ λόγος, ἀλλά τινος, τουτέστι τῆς ἐμμελοῦς. ἐμμελῆ δὲ φωνὴν τὴν αὐτὴν τῇ διαστηματικῇ τιθέμενος. ὅθεν δυνάμει τὸ λεγόμενον μέν ἐστι φωνῆς διαστηματικῆς. διαστηματικὴ δὲ φωνή ἐστιν ἡ πρὸς μέλος ἐπιτήδειος, ἣν διαστέλλονται πρὸς τὴν κατὰ τὰς ὁμιλίας εἰς τὴν χρῆσιν παραλαμβανομένην, ἣν συνεχῆ τε καὶ λογικὴν καλεῖν εἴωθεν ὁ Ἀριστόξενος. πτῶσις δὲ διὰ τὸ τὴν μὲν συνεχῆ ὡσανεὶ ἑστῶσαν εἶναι, τὴν μέντοι διαστηματικὴν τὴν ὀρθότητα μὴ σώζουσαν κεκλᾶσθαι, καὶ μονονουχὶ ἀπὸ τοῦ ἑστάναι πεσοῦσαν, ἐμμελῆ γεγονέναι. διὸ καὶ τὸ μέλος ἀποδιδόασι κλᾶσιν φωνῆς. . . . . τὸ δ' ἐπὶ μίαν τάσιν, ἐπεὶ τὸ μὲν ὅλον μέλος πτῶσίς ἐστιν ἐπὶ πολλὰς τάσεις, καὶ τοσαύτας ὅσας ἐν ἑαυτῷ

περιέχει κατὰ τὸ σύστημα. ὁ δὲ φθόγγος, ἕν τι μέρος ἐλα-
χιστον ὢν τοῦ μέλους, ἐξ ἀνάγκης καὶ τὴν ἐφ' ἑαυτὸν γενομένην
πτῶσιν μίαν ἔχει. . . . . ὅπερ οὖν παρὰ τοῖς Ἀριστοξενίοις
ἀπεδόθη, τὸ εἶναι τὸν φθόγγον φωνῆς ἐμμελοῦς πτῶσιν κατὰ
μίαν τάσιν ἐκφερομένην, τοῦτο μετείληπται εἰς τὸ εἶναι τὸν
φθόγγον ψόφον ἕνα καὶ τὸν αὐτὸν ἐπέχοντα τόνον.

Aristides Quintilianus, de musica, p. 9,2 Meib.: πᾶσα μὲν
οὖν ἁπλῆ κίνησις φωνῆς, τάσις. ἡ δὲ τῆς μελῳδικῆς, φθόγγος
ἰδίως καλεῖται.

Ibid., p. 9,17: φθόγγος μὲν οὖν ἐστι φωνῆς ἐμμελοῦς μέρος
ἐλάχιστον.

Cleonides (Pseudo-Euclid) also uses τάσις in the sense of
a musical sound. After defining the κίνησις φωνῆς συνεχής
and διαστηματική in the same terms as Aristoxenus, he says
(introd., 2, p. 2 Meib. (p. 180 K. v. J.)) that the rests (μοναί) in
the latter motion are called τάσεις, and continues, καλοῦνται
δὲ αἱ τάσεις καὶ φθόγγοι.

Gaudentius, harmonica introductio, 2, p. 3 Meib. (p. 329 K.
v. J.): φθόγγος δέ ἐστι φωνῆς πτῶσις ἐπὶ μίαν τάσιν· τάσις
δὲ μονὴ καὶ στάσις τῆς φωνῆς. ὅταν οὖν ἡ φωνὴ κατὰ μίαν
τάσιν ἑστάναι δόξῃ, τότε φαμὲν φθόγγον εἶναι τὴν φωνὴν οἷον
εἰς μέλος τάττεσθαι.

Some of the authors of treatises modify the definition of
Aristoxenus by adding ἐμμελής, as Porphyry (see above,
p. 28) reports the Aristoxeneans to have done.

Bacchius, introd. artis mus., I. 4, pp. 1, 2 Meib. (p. 292 K.
v. J.): Φθόγγος δὲ καθόλου τί ἐστι ; Φωνῆς ἐμμελοῦς πτῶσις
ἐπὶ μίαν τάσιν. μία γὰρ τάσις ἐν φωνῇ ληφθεῖσα ἐμμελῆ
φθόγγον ἀποτελεῖ.

Cleonides (Ps.-Euclid), introd.,1. p. 1 Meib.(p.179 K. v. J.):
φθόγγος μὲν οὖν ἐστι φωνῆς πτῶσις ἐμμελὴς ἐπὶ μίαν τάσιν.

Bryennius, harm., I. iv., p. 377,9 Wallis: Φθόγγος ἐστὶ
φωνῆς πτῶσις ἐμμελὴς ἐπὶ μίαν τάσιν, ἤτοι φωνὴ διαστηματα-
τική.

The addition of the word ἐμμελής introduces an element
which does not really belong to the notion of the musical

sound apart from its connection with other musical sounds. The terms ἐμμελής and ἐκμελής, used both of notes themselves and of the intervals formed by the notes, signify that they are usable or unusable in the same piece of music. One note is ἐκμελής with regard to another note, if the interval between them is not one which can occur in actual music, although it might be used in speech. For example, a note which should divide the interval of a semitone into two small intervals would be ἐκμελής in modern European music. Ptolemy divides φθόγγοι into the two classes οἱ ἐμμελεῖς and οἱ ἐκμελεῖς.

Ptolemy, *Harm.*, I. iv., p. 9 Wallis: εἰσὶ δὲ ἐμμελεῖς μὲν ὅσοι συναπτόμενοι πρὸς ἀλλήλους εὔφωνοι (or εὔφοροι) τυγχάνουσι πρὸς ἀκοήν. ἐκμελεῖς δὲ ὅσοι μὴ οὕτως ἔχουσι. Compare Porphyry, *commentarius*, p. 265 Wallis, and p. 215.

Gaudentius, after speaking of the two kinds of φωνή, the συνεχής and the διαστηματική, says (*harm. introd.*, 1, p. 2 Meib. (p. 328 K. v. J.)): ἰδίως δὲ τῆς διαστηματικῆς τὸ μὲν ἐμμελές, τὸ δὲ ἐκμελές· τὸ μὲν ῥητοῖς χρώμενον διαστήμασι καὶ μηδὲν ἀπολειπόμενον ἢ ὑπερβάλλον αὐτὸ ἐμμελές, τὸ δὲ ἐνδεὲς ἢ ὑπερβάλλον μικρῷ τῶν ὡρισμένων διαστημάτων ἐκμελές. And further on (*ibid.*, 3, p. 4 Meib. (p. 330, ιι K. v. J.)): τῶν δὲ διαστημάτων τὰ μέν ἐστιν ἐμμελῆ, τὰ δ' ἐκμελῆ. τῶν δ' ἐμμελῶν τὰ μὲν σύμφωνα, τὰ δὲ ἀσύμφωνα, κτέ.

These terms are then more appropriately applied to the intervals than to the notes, for it is evident that every conceivable degree of pitch can be used in melody if the key-note be suitably pitched.[1]

The term ἐμμελής is also used in nearly the same sense as διαστηματικός as opposed to συνεχής (see above, p. 18).

---

[1] It should be observed that sometimes only those φθόγγοι ἐμμελεῖς which are not consonant are included under the term. This narrower use is found in Ptolemy's *Harmonics*, I. vii., p. 15 Wallis, where ἀνισότονοι καὶ διωρισμένοι φθόγγοι are either ὁμόφωνοι or σύμφωνοι (two kinds of consonance are here distinguished) or ἐμμελεῖς.

See Porphyry, *l. c.* (p. 28, 26). In Bacchius φθόγγοι ἐμμελεῖς are opposed to φθόγγοι πεζοί.

Bacchius, *introd.*, II 69, pp. 16, 17 Meib. (p. 307 K. v. J.):
Φθόγγων δὲ πόσα λέγομεν εἶναι γένη ;—Δύο. τούτων δὲ οὓς μὲν ἐμμελεῖς καλοῦμεν, οὓς δὲ πεζούς.
Ἐμμελεῖς ποῖοί εἰσιν ;—Οἷς οἱ ᾄδοντες χρῶνται καὶ οἱ διὰ τῶν ὀργάνων τι ἐνεργοῦντες. τούτου γὰρ μὴ ὑπάρχοντος ἀδύνατόν τι τῶν κατὰ μουσικὴν δεῖξαι.
Πεζοὶ δὲ ποῖοί εἰσιν ;—Οἷς οἱ ῥήτορες χρῶνται καὶ οἷς αὐτοὶ πρὸς ἀλλήλους λαλοῦμεν. καὶ οἱ μὲν ἐμμελεῖς ὡρισμένα ἔχουσι τὰ διαστήματα, οἱ δὲ πεζοὶ ἀόριστα.

Other definitions of the musical sound given by Bryennius (see above) are : (p. 377,17) ἡ φθόγγος ἐστὶ φωνῆς ἐναρμόνιος τάσις. (p. 377,п) ἡ σαφέστερον εἰπεῖν φθόγγος ἐστὶ μιᾶς χορδῆς ποιά τις ἀπήχησις.[1]

---

[1] We may tabulate these definitions of the φθόγγος as follows :

Aristoxenus,	φωνῆς		πτῶσις	ἐπὶ	μίαν	τάσιν.
Gaudentius,	„		„	„	„	„
Bacchius,	„	ἐμμελοῦς	„	„	„	„
Aristoxeneans } (in Porph.), }	„	„	„	„ (κατὰ) „	„	(ἐκφερομένη).
	„	ἐμμελὴς	„	„	„	„
Cleonides,	„	„	„	„	„	„
Bryennius,	„	„	„	„	„	„
(Nicomachus),	„		ἐπίπτωσις „	„	„	καὶ ἁπλῆν.
Nicomachus,	„	ἐμμελοῦς	ἁπλατὴς	τάσις.		
Thrasyllus,	„	ἐναρμονίου		„		
Bryennius,	„	ἐναρμόνιος		„		
Aristides Quint.,	„	μελῳδικῆς		ἁπλῆ κίνησις.		
„ „	„	ἐμμελοῦς		μέρος ἐλάχιστον.		
Porphyry,		τοῦ μέλους	ἕν τι	„	„	
Ptolemy,	ψόφος		ἕνα καὶ τὸν αὐτὸν τόνον ἐπέχων.			
Pythagoreans } (in Porph.), }	„		παρὰ μίαν τάσιν ἐκφερόμενος.			
Bryennius,	φωνὴ		διαστηματική.			
Nicomachus,	„		ἄτομος.			
(Nicomachus),	ἦχος		ἁπλατὴς κατὰ τόπον ἀδιάστατος.			
Bryennius,	ἀπήχησις		ποιά τις μιᾶς χορδῆς.			

Two notes or musical sounds are said to form an interval
when they differ in pitch; or, an interval is the difference or
distance in pitch between two notes.
The definitions of interval in the Greek musical treatises
will now be quoted.

Aristoxenus, *Harm.*, I. § 37, p. 15 Meib.: διάστημα δ' ἐστὶ
τὸ ὑπὸ δύο φθόγγων ὡρισμένον μὴ τὴν αὐτὴν τάσιν ἐχόντων.
φαίνεται γὰρ, ὡς τύπῳ εἰπεῖν, διαφορά τις εἶναι τάσεων τὸ
διάστημα καὶ τόπος δεκτικὸς φθόγγων ὀξυτέρων μὲν τῆς βαρυτέρας τῶν ὁριζουσῶν τὸ διάστημα τάσεων, βαρυτέρων δὲ τῆς
ὀξυτέρας.

Thrasyllus apud Theonem Smyrnaeum, *de musica*, c. 3, p.
48 Hiller: διάστημα δέ φησιν εἶναι φθόγγων τὴν πρὸς ἀλλήλους ποιὰν σχέσιν, οἷον διὰ τεσσάρων, διὰ πέντε, διὰ πασῶν.

Plutarch, *de animae procreatione*, xvii., 1020 E: ἔστι γὰρ
διάστημα ἐν μελῳδίᾳ πᾶν τὸ περιεχόμενον ὑπὸ δυοῖν φθόγγων
ἀνομοίων τῇ τάσει.

Ptolemy does not seem to give a definition of interval unless
one is contained in the following words.

Ptolemy, *Harm.*, I. iii., p. 7 Wallis: ἔοικεν ἡ κατὰ τὸ ὀξὺ
καὶ βαρὺ τῶν ψόφων διαφορὰ ποσότητος εἶδος εἶναί τι.

Aelian in Porphyry, *commentarius in Ptolemaeum*, p. 217
Wallis: συμφανὲς ὅτι ὀξὺς φθόγγος ἀπὸ τοῦ βαρυτέρου
διάστημα ἀφέστηκεν· καὶ ἡ διαφορὰ τοῦ ὀξυτέρου παρὰ τὸν
βαρύτερον φθόγγον, καὶ τοῦ βαρυτέρου παρὰ τὸν ὀξύτερον
καλεῖται διάστημα. (p. 218) καὶ οὕτως ὁρίζεται τὸ διάστημα·
δυοῖν φθόγγων ἀνομοίων ὀξύτητι καὶ βαρύτητι διαφέρον.

Nicomachus, *harmonices manuale*, 4, pp. 7, 8 Meib. (p. 243
K.v.J.): διάστημα δὲ ὁδὸν ποιὰν ἀπὸ βαρύτητος εἰς ὀξύτητα
ἢ ἀνάπαλιν.

Ibid., 12, p. 24 Meib. (p. 261 K.v.J.): διάστημα δ' ἐστὶ
δυοῖν φθόγγων μεταξύτης.

Bacchius Senior, *introductio*, p. 2 Meib. (p. 292 K.v.J.):
Διάστημα δὲ τί ἐστι;—Διαφορὰ δύο φθόγγων ἀνομοίων ὀξύτητι καὶ βαρύτητι.

Cleonides, *introductio*, 1, p. 1 Meib. (p. 179 K. v. J.): διάστημα δὲ τὸ περιεχόμενον ὑπὸ δύο φθόγγων ἀνομοίων ὀξύτητι καὶ βαρύτητι.
Ibid., 2, p. 2 Meib. (p. 180 K. v. J.): τὰς μὲν οὖν μονὰς τάσεις καλοῦμεν, τὰς δὲ μεταβάσεις τὰς ἀπὸ τάσεων ἐπὶ τάσεις διαστήματα.
Gaudentius, *harmon. introd.*, 3, p. 4 Meib. (p. 329 K. v. J.): διάστημα δέ ἐστι τὸ ὑπὸ δύο φθόγγων περιεχόμενον. ἡ τοίνυν διαφορὰ τοῦ ὀξυτέρου παρὰ τὸν βαρύτερον φθόγγον καὶ τοῦ βαρυτέρου παρὰ τὸν ὀξύτερον λέγοιτ᾽ ἂν διάστημα.

Bryennius has collected a great number of definitions, which he presents as alternatives.

Bryennius, *harm.*, I. sect. v., p. 381 Wallis: τὸ διάστημα τοίνυν διχῶς λέγεται· κοινῶς καὶ ἰδίως. καὶ κοινῶς μὲν πᾶν μέγεθος τὸ ὑπό τινων περάτων ὁριζόμενον. ἰδίως δὲ κατὰ τὴν μουσικὴν ὅπερ οὕτως ὁρίζεται, διάστημά ἐστι μέγεθος φωνῆς ὑπὸ δυοῖν φθόγγων περιγεγραμμένον· ἡ διάστημά ἐστι τὸ περιεχόμενον ὑπὸ δύο φθόγγων ἀνομοίων τῇ τάσει ἤτοι ὀξύτητι καὶ βαρύτητι· ἡ ὁδὸς ποιὰ ἀπὸ βαρύτητος εἰς ὀξύτητα ἡ ἀνάπαλιν· ἡ διάστημά ἐστι τὸ ὑπὸ δύο φθόγγων ὡρισμένον μὴ τὴν αὐτὴν ἐχόντων τάσιν· ἤτοι διαφορά τις τάσεων καὶ τόπος δεκτικὸς φθόγγων, ὀξυτέρων μὲν τῆς βαρυτέρας τῶν ὁριζουσῶν τὸ διάστημα τάσεων, βαρυτέρων δὲ τῆς ὀξυτέρας· διαφορὰ δέ ἐστι τάσεων τὸ μᾶλλον καὶ ἧττον τετάσθαι· ἡ διάστημά ἐστι δυοῖν φθόγγων ἡ πρὸς ἀλλήλους ποιὰ σχέσις.

For the sake of bringing out more clearly the differences in the definitions which have just been quoted, we may group them in classes. The musical interval is defined in one of the following manners :

(1) a certain *relation* between two musical sounds (Thrasyllus, Bryennius).

(2) a *difference* of pitches (Aristoxenus, Bryennius) ; or the difference between an acute and a grave sound or between two sounds not of the same pitch (Ptolemy, Aelian, Bacchius, Gaudentius).

4

(3) that which is *bounded* or *encompassed* by two sonds not of the same pitch (Aristoxenus, Plutarch, Cleonides, Claudentius, Bryennius); or a region or space (τόπος) receptre of sounds intermediate in pitch to the bounding sounds (Aristoxenus, Bryennius); or a vocal magnitude defined or bouded by two sounds (Bryennius).

(4) a *passage* (ὁδός or μετάβασις) from acute to grve or *vice versâ* or from one pitch to another (Nicomachus, Cleoides, Bryennius).

Dismissing definition (1) because it is too vague, we may notice that the definitions in group (2) merely express the fact that it is a pitch-difference on which the relationship depends, but do not imply that there is such a thing as difference in the size of intervals and that measurement is possible. The difference of pitches might be like a difference in color, or in dors or tastes. In the definitions numbered (3) the idea of a pace or distance is clearly brought out, and in (4) the notio of movement from one bound to the other is included. Both (3) and (4) imply more or less clearly the infinite subdivisibility of pitch. This is very plain in the definition that an interval is a space receptive of intermediate pitches, for an intermediate pitch would form two new smaller intervals, which would themselves also be divisible into yet smaller intervals. 1 4), and to a certain extent also in (3), κίνησις συνεχής seen to lie at the bottom of the conception of an interval. Without this idea of a gradual passage from one pitch to another, is hard to see how change of pitch could be regarded as a passge at all. If the pitch changes suddenly, in the way indiced by κίνησις διαστηματική, the sensation does not sugget a transition or transference so much as a transformation. The effect is similar to that produced by a sudden change in cor. Intermediate shades of color are not present to the mind.

The continuous nature of pitch would naturally be on of the earliest points to be observed. But, although it wold readily be admitted that to all intents and purposes puch seemed to be a continuous quantity and not a discrete quan-

ty, when the question of finding a *means of measuring* differ-
nce of pitch was presented, it would be natural to endeavor
1 find a smallest possible interval which might serve as a
ntural unit.

We have in Plato a reference to such attempts.

Plato, *Republic*, VII., p. 530 E: ἡ οὐκ οἶσθ᾽ ὅτι καὶ περὶ
ρμονίας ἕτερον τοιοῦτον ποιοῦσι; τὰς γὰρ ἀκουομένας αὖ
υμφωνίας καὶ φθόγγους ἀλλήλοις ἀναμετροῦντες ἀνήνυτα
ωσπερ οἱ ἀστρονόμοι πονοῦσι. νὴ τοὺς θεούς, ἔφη, καὶ γε-
λοίως γε, πυκνώματ᾽ ἄττα ὀνομάζοντες καὶ παραβάλλοντες τὰ
τα, οἷον ἐκ γειτόνων φωνὴν θηρευόμενοι, οἱ μέν φασιν ἔτι
ατακούειν ἐν μέσῳ τινὰ ἠχὴν καὶ σμικρότατον εἶναι τοῦτο
ιάστημα, ᾧ μετρητέον, οἱ δὲ ἀμφισβητοῦντες ὡς ὅμοιον ἤδη
ὑθεγγομένων, ἀμφότεροι ὦτα τοῦ νοῦ προστησάμενοι. (Quoted
in Theo Smyrnaeus, p. 6 Hiller.)

But it is evident that in dealing with the sensation of pitch
there is the widest range for differences of opinion, and even
if a considerable number of competent persons could agree
that some given interval was the smallest difference of pitch
which they could distinguish from unison, there would still
exist the necessity for finding a method of recording the
width of this interval, and this record must necessarily rest
on physical considerations. Thus, in any exact method of
measurement, final appeal will always have to be made to the
intellect. The ear alone cannot be trusted to judge the width
of small dissonant intervals so accurately as to enable us to
measure larger intervals in terms of the smaller. When we
consider the difficulty of singing with accuracy the ordinary
chromatic scale, with intervals so large as semitones, the impossibility of obtaining certain results by means of the ear
alone will be apparent.

If, now, the attempt to find **by ear a** minute interval to
serve **as a** unit in measuring intervallar size is doomed to
failure, it naturally occurs to inquire if it is possible to select
for the unit one of the intervals found in actual use in music.
Although the number of such intervals (called by the Greeks

ἐμμελῆ) [1] is very small compared with the number of intervals possible,[2] it does not seem unreasonable to hope that one or other of them, or some aliquot part, may serve our purpose.

Suppose, now, that we represent pitch by a straight line, and that equal distances on the line stand for equal intervals, wherever taken. If then we arbitrarily choose a certain length on the line to represent any given interval, such as the Octave,[3] it will, of course, be possible to find distances which will accurately represent all other intervals. The sum of two such distances will then represent the sum of the two corresponding intervals, obtained by making the acute note of one of them coincide with the grave note of the other. In like manner the arithmetical difference of any two distances will represent the difference of the corresponding intervals, obtained by making the two acute notes or the two grave notes coincide.

---

[1] See above, p. 30.

[2] Compare Sedley Taylor, *Sight Singing*, §§ 11, 12, where it is stated that within the compass of an average voice, two or three hundred different degrees of pitch are distinguishable. If the compass of such a voice is taken to be an octave and a fifth (*op. cit.* § 74), only twenty of these different pitches are found on our keyed instruments, where temperament prevails. This number is considerably increased in practice, when temperament is ignored, as in singing and violin music, but even then the number of notes to the octave is comparatively small. It must be remembered that in those computations in which it is found that a perfect keyed instrument would have to have twenty-five or more keys within each octave, many of these notes are incompatible (so to speak) with one another (ἐκμελεῖς). Belonging to remotely related keys, they do not occur in one and the same piece of music, and are often so close as to be almost indistinguishable in pitch. It is equally true of Greek music, that, although a large number of notes within each octave was recognized, they were not all of them usable in the same piece of music. Aristoxenus (*Harm.*, p. 28 Meib.) is our authority for the statement that the voice cannot advance by quarter-tones beyond the second step. The number of notes used at one time was never many more than eight within the octave.

[3] Following the example of Mr. A. J. Ellis in his translation of Helmholtz's *Sensations of Tone*, 2nd. Eng. ed., 1885, the names of *intervals* will hereafter be written with capital initial letters, as Fifth, Major-third, Semitone.

The question before us is then equivalent to the following : Are these linear distances commensurable or incommensurable?[1] The answer must here be given without proof, although its truth is susceptible of mathematical demonstration. It is that not one of the more usual intervals found in actual music is commensurable with any other, nor is it possible to find an interval of any size that will not be incommensurable with almost every interval which, from its occurrence in music, we might desire to measure.

Intervals like the Octave, Fifth, Major-tone, etc., which the ear recognizes as having a special claim to a name and place in every musical system, are all incommensurable with one another. No two distances (on the line of pitch) corresponding to intervals of actual occurrence in natural music can be expressed in terms of a common unit.[2] Nor can any distance be discovered, however small or large, which will serve our purpose with any greater success.

The cause for this state of affairs is found in the well-known fact that all intervals are expressible in terms of ratios, which are derived from physical phenomena. As has been noticed before (p. 14), pitch depends on the number of vibrations of the air generated in any period of time by the cause of the sound. The ratio between the vibration-numbers of two notes expresses the size of the interval. Since, now, to compound two ratios it is necessary to multiply them together,

---

[1] Two quantities are commensurable when there is a third quantity which is contained an exact number of times in each.

[2] One or two evident exceptions need cause no trouble in accepting the essential truth of this doctrine. The Double Octave and the Double Fifth (= Octave + Major-tone), for example, are obviously twice the size of the single Octave and Fifth, respectively Again, after selecting a unit (for example, the Tone) nothing can prevent us from *constructing* intervals of twice or any number of times the size, as the Pythagorean Major-third (see below, p. 38); but the resulting intervals in this latter case are not truly musical intervals, but are generally approximations to natural intervals. Of this more will be said on p. 47.

and not, of course, to add them, it follows that the sum of two intervals cannot be obtained by direct addition of their ratios, nor are ratios so related that a common constituent can be found which could serve as a measure of their relative size. "If we wish to have a measure of intervals in the proper sense, we must take, not the characteristic ratio itself, but the logarithm of that ratio. Then, and then only, will the measure of a compound interval be the *sum* of the measures of the components,"[1] and when this has been done all the logarithms, with a few exceptions, will be found to be incommensurable. But of course, the size of any interval can be calculated to any required degree of accuracy.

This great fact of the incommensurability of musical intervals was known to the Greeks. It was recognized to be true both practically and theoretically. The eleventh chapter of the first book of Ptolemy's *Harmonics* contains first a mathematical demonstration that six Tones exceed an Octave, and the amount of this excess, it is then stated, is perceptible *even to the ear*. Earlier writers than Ptolemy prove mathematically that six Tones exceed an Octave by an interval (called the Pythagorean Comma) whose ratio is 524,288 : 531,441. Since this excess is slightly larger than the Comma of Didymus (80 : 81) which is the difference between the Major and the Minor Whole-tone (or between the true or just Major-third and the Pythagorean Major-third), Ptolemy's statement is not in the least incredible. All the difficulties sought to be obviated by the device of equal temperament arise from small intervals, which are rarely larger than the Comma (80 : 81) by even a quarter of its size. If such intervals are felt by moderns, we cannot deny to the ancients ability to perceive small intervals of the same size. The existence of Quarter-tones at one period, at least, in the development of Greek music, points to a high degree of cultivation among the ancients of the feeling for pitch-differences.

---

[1] Lord Rayleigh, *The Theory of Sound* (1894), Vol. I, p. 7.

Again, the Pythagorean School of musical theorists, more mathematically inclined than their opponents, the Aristoxeneans, consistently denied that the Fifth and Fourth were equal to $3\frac{1}{2}$ and $2\frac{1}{2}$ Tones respectively. But as in modern theory these incontrovertible facts are often consciously or unconsciously ignored, so in the ancient musical world we find the Aristoxenean School using the Semitone, defined as half of the Whole-tone (which in turn is defined as the difference between the Fifth and the Fourth) as a unit for the measurement of all other intervals. It is inconvenient, to say the least, to have no unit supplied by nature, and for the purposes of a practical notation some sort of an approximate unit would seem to be almost a necessity for a music developed to the point of demanding different keys and modes. In teaching, moreover, it is very desirable to be able to regard that scale (with us the chromatic) in which progression is made by the smallest steps recognized, as composed of equal-sized intervals.

For rougher measurements, then, we are fully justified in assuming as a unit whatever interval we find most convenient for the purpose. The size of such an interval will, of course, depend on the nature of the music concerned. Thus in Hindu Music the Octave is regarded as consisting of 22 small intervals (çrutis), such that nine of them make a Fourth and thirteen a Fifth, and consequently four make the Major Whole-tone. In Arabian Music 17 approximately equal intervals compose the Octave. But ancient Greek Music, like modern European Music, recognizes an Octave of 12 nominally equal small intervals (ἡμιτόνια, Semitones) of which five make up the Fourth and seven the Fifth and two the Tone, which is their difference. They are, however, unlike in this, that, while in modern Music no interval differing very widely from the twelfth part of an Octave or some multiple thereof is used, in ancient Greek Music, on the contrary, the existence at various periods of Quarter- and Third-tones (equal to one-half and two-thirds of the Semitone respectively) is well attested. For this reason the Tone is perhaps a better unit for rough measurement than the Semitone. Whether or not the subtle refinements known as Chroai, which were varieties of the quarter-tone system (*genus enharmonicum*) and of the third-tone system (*genus chromaticum*), corresponded to phenomena actually observed, the fact remains that Greek theoretical writers used thirtieths and even sixtieths of the Fourth in their explanations of these various *genera*. These intervals would then be twelfths and twenty-fourths of a compromise Tone obtained by taking exactly two-fifths of a Fourth. It is easy to see that a mean Tone of this size is not equal to an equal-temperament Tone, because a Fourth falls short of five equal-temperament Semitones, and consequently two-fifths of a Fourth fall short of an 'equal' Tone. Moreover, this mean Tone, depending as it does on the Fourth, like the Fourth, is not an aliquot part of the Octave. In like manner neither the thirtieth nor the sixtieth part of a Fourth is an aliquot part of the Octave. In their more accurate measurements of intervals the Greeks used the Fourth as a standard of length, where moderns use the Octave. In this respect and in some others the Fourth played the part now taken by the Octave. For rougher calculations, as we have seen, the Tone and the Semitone—sixth and twelfth of the Octave respectively—were used. But the most perfect of all the methods is that in which the size of intervals is determined by the ratio [1] between the numbers found to belong to the notes.

---

[1] Ratio is defined by Euclid in the following words (Euclid, *Elements*, v. def. 3): "Ratio is a mutual relation of two magnitudes of the same kind to one another in respect of quantity," or rather of "quantuplicity." It is immaterial which of the two magnitudes first receives the attention of the mind. It is also a matter of indifference which term of a ratio is regarded as compared with the other, whether the larger is compared with the smaller or the smaller with the larger, provided one or the other method is consistently adhered to during one and the same operation. It is usual to consider the term first mentioned to be compared with the term last mentioned, as 2 to 3, *i. e.*, 2 compared with 3. But if we wish to compare two ratios, as 2:3 and 5:7, to see which is the larger or wider, we may either take the antecedents, 2 and 5, as standards, and so proceed to change the

Pythagoras[1] is accredited with making the discovery of the numerical relations existing between musical sounds, and the Pythagorean School[2] always made ratio the basis of their investigations. They demonstrated[3] by the use of ratios that certain intervals are not divisible into exactly equal parts. This would seem to show that they appreciated the difficulties connected with the 'linear' measurement of intervals (so to call it), and knew that the majority of musical intervals are incommensurable with one another in respect of their size. But in the ratios they found a method of measuring intervals in which the difficulties caused by this characteristic feature in the constitution of musical intervals do not obtrude themselves.

Given any two notes, their interval may be calculated by finding the vibration-numbers and deducing the ratio. But the ancients are not known to have had any satisfactory means

---

terms of the ratios until the antecedents are the same, and then compare the consequents (thus, $2:3 = 10:15$ and $5:7 = 10:14$, therefore $2:3$ is wider, because 15 is larger than 14), or we may regard the consequents, 3 and 7, as standards of comparison and compare $14:21$ with $15:21$. The latter method is more usual, because ratios may be regarded as fractions. The consequents then become denominators, and the fractions are compared by reducing to a common denominator and comparing the numerators ($\frac{2}{3} = \frac{14}{21}$; $\frac{5}{7} = \frac{15}{21}$). But it would be just as legitimate to reduce the numerators to a common numerator, 10, and then to compare the denominators, 15 and 14 ($\frac{2}{3} = \frac{10}{15}$; $\frac{5}{7} = \frac{10}{14}$).

[1] We have the following statement of Xenocrates, as quoted by Heraclides Ponticus. The passage is found in an excerpt from Heraclides' Εἰσαγωγὴ Μουσικῆ given by Porphyry.

Porphyry, comm. in Ptol., I. iii. init., p. 213 Wallis: Πυθαγόρας, ἅς φησι Ξενοκράτης, εὕρισκε καὶ τὰ ἐν μουσικῇ διαστήματα οὐ χωρὶς ἀριθμοῦ τὴν γένεσιν ἔχοντα· ἔστι γὰρ σύγκρισις ποσοῦ πρὸς ποσόν.

Cf. Macrobius, comm. in somn. Scipionis, II. i. 8 sq., and Jan's note; Diogenes Laertius, viii. 11; Bryennius, I. i., p. 361 Wallis; Gevaert, Histoire et Théorie de la Musique de l'Antiquité, I. p. 74; Westphal, Rhythmik u. Harmonik, p. 62; Musik, p. 176; K. v. Jan, Mus. Scr. Gr., p. 53.

[2] See K. v. Jan, Mus. Scr. Gr., pp. 120–146, on the doctrines of the Pythagoreans.

[3] E. g. Euclid, sectio canonis, § 16, p. 35 Meib. (p. 161 K. v. J.).

either for counting the number of vibrations or for accurately measuring small intervals of time like the second. Consequently ancient determinations of the ratios of intervals were generally based on other considerations. The most convenient method consisted of a comparison of the lengths of the strings which produce the required notes, when the strings are made of a uniform thickness and are subjected to the same tension. As it happens, the lengths of strings are inversely proportional to their vibration-numbers, so that results obtained by one method may readily be compared with those obtained by the other. This is most easily done when two notes only are involved, but the comparison is made without difficulty even when there is a series of notes. Other methods employed were the comparison of the lengths of the pipes of wind instruments of equal bore; the comparison of the distances at which finger-holes must be bored to produce given notes; and the comparison of the weights necessary to stretch strings of equal length as well as size, so as to produce notes which will form the required interval.[1] Only very rough results could have been obtained from the methods last mentioned. In the case of instruments like the flute ($a\dot{v}\lambda\acute{o}\varsigma$) it is very difficult to determine accurately the length of the vibrating column of air, and it is necessary that the bore of the instrument be of uniform size throughout and that the size of the finger-holes be the same. A hole of smaller diameter may be substituted for one of larger diameter further removed from the mouth-piece. Ancient flute-makers undoubtedly availed themselves of this principle in tuning their instruments.[2] For ascertaining interval ratios by measuring the distances at which the holes are placed it would be necessary to have holes of one size only.

In using strings of equal length and thickness, stretched by hanging weights of different sizes, great care would have to be

[1] Cf. Theon. Smyrn., de musica, c. 12, p. 57 Hiller.
[2] See A. A. Howard in Harvard Studies, IV., The Aὐλός, p. 2.

exercised. For in order that two strings of equal length and size shall produce sounds which form some given interval, it is necessary to use weights which are to each other inversely as the *squares* of the lengths of strings of equal size at the same tension producing the same interval; in other words, the lengths vary inversely as the square-roots of the weights. The weights would not, therefore, give directly the ratios desired. It is doubtful if the ancients could have obtained the musical ratios from weights attached to strings. Allowance would also have to be made for the fact that the weight of the string per linear unit is diminished by the tension. Ptolemy appreciated the difficulties attending these methods and discusses them in his *Harmonics*, I. viii., p. 17 Wallis.

The instrument on which the greatest reliance was placed for determining the ratios was the κανὼν μονόχορδος or ἁρμονικός. Ptolemy describes it in the chapter cited above. It consisted of a vibrating string stretched between two fixed bridges, and passing over a third bridge, which could move freely between the fixed bridges, and thus could be used to divide the whole length of the string into two parts at any desired point. The distance between the movable bridge and the fixed bridges was measured on a scale which ran beneath the string. By means of this instrument the ratios associated with the various musical intervals could easily be calculated. Conversely, if the movable bridge were placed at such a point that the distance from one fixed bridge bore a certain ratio to the length of the whole string, the interval corresponding to the ratio could be produced. If the whole length of the string were tuned to be in unison with the lowest note of the scale of two Octaves, called the Perfect System, the proper distances could be marked off for all the other notes. This operation was called ἡ τοῦ κανόνος κατατομή. We have a description of the method in which the string was divided to produce this scale in Theo Smyrnaeus, *de musica*, c. 12 (pp. 57, 58 Hiller), and cc. 35, 36 (pp. 87–93 Hiller), where Thrasyllus is quoted *in extenso*; and in Euclid, *sectio canonis*, §§ 19, 20 (p. 163, sq.

K. v. J.).[1] The important feature of the monochord is that the tension of the parts of the string is necessarily the same as that of the whole string. The element of tension is thus eliminated.

The intervals to which attention would naturally first be directed in investigations into the ratios are the consonant intervals. The terms consonant and dissonant refer, of course, to the character of the intervals in regard to the smoothness or roughness of the combination of sounds. By far the greater number of possible intervals are dissonant. A small number of certain definite sizes or widths are consonant. In the matter of size they seem to bear no particular relation with one another and with dissonant intervals. As we have seen,[2] they are incommensurable quantities. As to their consonance, they vary markedly among themselves, and the smoothness of the same consonant interval will vary according to the absolute position of the combination in the scale of acuteness and graveness and according to the timbre of the notes. But at the same time each consonant interval can always be recognized with ease and certainty, and, moreover, is fixed in point of size within narrow limits by reason of the physical causes of the consonance. Such intervals are especially adapted to investigations into the relations which exist between the vibration-numbers, and between the lengths of the vibrating strings and of the columns of air producing the notes.

In regard to the number of consonances and the question of classifying intervals as consonant or dissonant, it is unnecessary here to name the intervals regarded by the Greeks as consonant, except to state that the number of consonant intervals varied from time to time, but was always considerably less than the number recognized in modern theory. Many of the

---

[1] See Boeckh, *De Metris Pindari*, lib. iii. c. vii. (*Pindari Opera*, tom. 1, pp. 209, 210); *Kleine Schriften*, iii., *Ueber die Bildung der Weltseele im Timaeos des Platon*, p. 66 (p. 150).

[2] See p. 37.

intervals now called imperfect consonances, although used in ancient music not only in melody (note after note), but also in accompaniment or harmony (note against note), were nevertheless classed as dissonant.

But there are three intervals which are consonant to so marked a degree that they are classed as consonant in every musical system. They are the Octave, the Fifth, and the Fourth. Inasmuch as all the other intervals which the Greek treatises recognize as consonant may be derived from these three primary consonances, and consist of two or more of them added together,[1] it will be sufficient if we show that the ratios belonging to these three intervals were discovered by the ancients, and that this important method of measuring intervals was successfully employed by them. We shall then have an absolutely trustworthy means of identifying ancient intervals with their modern representatives.

Pythagoras, honored by the Greeks as the discoverer of the musical ratios, determined the ratio for the Octave ($\delta\iota\grave{\alpha}\ \pi\alpha\sigma\hat{\omega}\nu$) to be $1:2$, the ratio for the Fifth ($\delta\iota\grave{\alpha}\ \pi\acute{\epsilon}\nu\tau\epsilon$ or $\delta\iota'\ \grave{o}\xi\epsilon\iota\hat{\omega}\nu$) to be $2:3$, and the ratio for the Fourth ($\delta\iota\grave{\alpha}\ \tau\epsilon\sigma\sigma\acute{\alpha}\rho\omega\nu$) to be $3:4$; that is to say, a string whose length is double that of another sounds a note an Octave lower, and similarly with the other intervals. These ratios were undoubtedly obtained by direct observation. We may suppose the philosopher to have used either a single string, furnished with a finger-board, or two strings tuned in unison, or a string furnished with a movable bridge as described above (p. 43), the monochord. The lyre is not adapted to such experiments, but the Egyptians had instruments with very long strings stretched over a finger-board, and Pythagoras may easily have been acquainted with these. The ratios

---

[1] It is true that the Octave is equal to the sum of the Fifth and Fourth, and all the Greek consonances may thus be said to be composed of Fifths and Fourths; but it is better for a number of reasons to regard the Fifth and the Fourth as parts of the Octave, the result of the first division thereof, than to regard the latter as the result of compounding the former.

of other intervals, consonant and dissonant, may have been obtained either directly from the string or indirectly by combining the ratios already found. Thus the consonant intervals, the Twelfth (Octave + Fifth) and the Double-octave, were probably found to depend on the ratios 1 : 3 and 1 : 4, respectively. The Tone, which is the difference in width between the Fifth and the Fourth, was certainly regarded as dependent on the ratio 8 : 9, but it is probable that this ratio was often deduced from the ratios already obtained, and was not directly observed from the lengths of string.

This fact, that the Tone is the difference of the two important consonances, the Fifth and the Fourth, has given this dissonant interval a prominent place in musical theory. In consequence of being defined in this manner (as the difference of two consonant intervals), the Tone may be tuned with the same degree of precision that is obtainable in the case of the consonant intervals. Dissonant intervals in general cannot be tuned with any great accuracy. The Tone is thus closely related to the consonances. Another fact has aided in giving the Tone an importance not rightfully belonging to it. It is that it differs from the sixth part of the Octave by only a minute interval. The ratio 8 : 9 taken six times (= 262,144 : 531,441) differs from the ratio 1 : 2 (= 262,144 : 524,288) by a very small ratio. The corresponding small interval, called the Pythagorean Comma, is only a little larger than the ordinary Comma (80 : 81), an interval which is neglected in the tuning of modern keyed instruments. For these two reasons the Tone seemed to be well adapted for use as a unit of measurement, and to have an especial quality. We are not, therefore, surprised to find that the Tone is of frequent occurrence in scales, as it is the only difference between intervals which were recognized as consonant, which was not itself also consonant. Its appearance in theoretical scales is natural; the facility with which it may be tuned would undoubtedly cause it also to appear in scales as actually tuned—for example, on the lyre. But, if it is permitted to draw conclusions by analogy from facts presented to us in the history of modern theory, it is not extravagant to suppose that intervals of nearly the same size as the Tone were often mistaken for the Tone, and that the Tone personated these intervals, so to speak. If there were intervals in ancient Greek scales whose size differed from that of the Tone in question by only a small amount (and the existence of such intervals is not only possible, but is distinctly asserted by many of the ancients), it would be a most natural error to suppose such intervals to be actual Tones and to call them Tones and to tune them as such on instruments. Yet they would not for all that be the same interval as the Tone, nor would they cease to be intoned according to the dictates of artistic feeling whenever the instrument permitted this to be done, as in vocal music. In modern music there are two intervals, approaching the Tone (more accurately called the Major-tone) in point of size, which are used quite as freely as it is. They are the Supersecond or Septimal-second (ratio 7:8) and the Minor-tone (ratio 9:10), one wider, the other narrower, than the Major-tone (ratio 8:9). These intervals can be accurately intoned in vocal and violin music, but on keyed instruments (with the usual number of keys) they are all three represented by the same tempered interval. The small inaccuracies are overlooked, and the intervals are all called Tones alike. A similar state of affairs may have existed in ancient music. Scales in which Major-tones predominate are open to suspicion on that account. In the next paragraph we shall see that the scale constructed in the *Timaeus* of Plato is artificial in this respect.

The earliest passage in which the consonant ratios are mentioned is perhaps Plato, *Timaeus*, 35 B, sq.[1] It is to be observed, however, that there is nowhere any reference to music in the text. The scale here constructed is essentially a theoretical one. The procedure is as follows. First, the

---

[1] See the notes on this passage in Archer-Hind, *The Timaeus of Plato*, p. 107, sq.

double geometrical quaternion or tetractys of the Pythagoreans is formed by joining to unity the first three powers of 2 and of 3, thus: 1, 2, 3, 4, 9, 8, 27. This tetractys may be arranged so as to exhibit the two branches consisting of powers of 2 and 3, respectively, by making a Lambda,[1] as follows:

$$1$$
$$2 \quad\quad 3$$
$$4 \quad\quad\quad 9$$
$$8 \quad\quad\quad\quad 27$$

The left branch contains the duple intervals (διπλάσια διαστήματα) and the right one the triple intervals (τριπλάσια διαστήματα). Then between the terms of every interval the harmonical[2] and the arithmetical means are inserted. In this way two series are obtained: 1, $\frac{4}{3}$, $\frac{3}{2}$, 2, $\frac{8}{3}$, 3, 4, $\frac{16}{3}$, 6, 8; and 1, $\frac{3}{2}$, 2, 3, $\frac{9}{2}$, 6, 9, $\frac{27}{2}$, 18, 27. The succession of intervals in the first series, or left branch, is $\frac{4}{3}$, $\frac{9}{8}$, $\frac{4}{3}$; $\frac{4}{3}$, $\frac{9}{8}$, $\frac{4}{3}$; $\frac{4}{3}$, $\frac{9}{8}$, $\frac{4}{3}$; the succession in the second series, or right branch, is $\frac{3}{2}$, $\frac{4}{3}$, $\frac{3}{2}$; $\frac{3}{2}$, $\frac{4}{3}$, $\frac{3}{2}$; $\frac{3}{2}$, $\frac{4}{3}$, $\frac{3}{2}$; that is to say, in the first series, the second term is $\frac{4}{3}$ of the first, the third $\frac{3}{2}$ of the second, etc. The explanation of these series is held by commentators to be that they refer to musical scales. The ratios $\frac{3}{2}$ and $\frac{4}{3}$ will then correspond to the consonances of the Fifth and the Fourth, their product ($\frac{3}{2} \times \frac{4}{3} = \frac{2}{1}$) to the sum of these intervals, the Octave, and their quotient ($\frac{3}{2} \div \frac{4}{3} = \frac{9}{8}$) to the difference, the Tone. The last step in the formation of the scales is that by which every interval of $4:3$ was filled with intervals of $9:8$ (as many as are contained therein), and λείμματα, whose terms are as 256 to 243, the intervals of $3:2$ being first resolved (by implication) into intervals of $4:3$ and $9:8$. Scales are therefore formed in which each note

---

[1] Attributed to Crantor (Plutarch, *de anim. procr.*, c. 29, 1027 D).

[2] The harmonical mean is such that the difference between it and the lesser extreme is the same part of the latter as the difference between the greater extreme and the harmonical mean is of that extreme.

49

differs from its neighbors by an interval of either 9 : 8 or
256 : 243, that is, every step is either a Tone or a Leimma.
The scale formed on the binary branch of the tetractys has a
compass of three Octaves, each Octave containing 5 Tones and
2 Leimmata. The scale formed on the ternary branch[1] has a
compass of three Twelfths, each Twelfth or Dodecachord being
of the form : nete diezeugmenon—mese—hypate meson—proslambanomenus,[2] in which the intervals are Fifth, Fourth,
Fifth, and form together an Octave like the Octave of the
binary scale, *plus* the interval of a Fifth towards the bass,
hypate meson—proslambanomenus. Each of the three Dodecachords, then, contains 8 Tones and 3 Leimmata, when
the scale is completed.

The fact that the compass of each of these scales is much
larger than that of any scale described in the musical treatises
goes far towards showing that they are not to be regarded
as actual musical scales.[3] In the ternary scale there is the
further objection that each of the three Dodecachords is in a
different key. In other words, the ternary scale passes into
two new keys.

The question, then, naturally occurs, Are these scales musical scales at all in the modern sense of the word musical? Do
they not rather belong to the music of numbers (ἡ ἐν ἀριθμοῖς
μουσική)? The ancient commentators on the passage themselves support this view. It is admitted by Adrastus, quoted
by Theo Smyrnaeus, *de musica*, c. 13 (p. 64, sq. Hiller), that
the compass of scales actually used in music falls far short of
that of the longer scale described by Plato, of which the
length is four Octaves and a Major-sixth (= three Twelfths);
but it is pointed out that it was necessary to extend the scale
into cubic numbers, because they represent solids.[4] In any

---

[1] Cf. Archer-Hind, *op. cit.*, p. 111, note.
[2] The names are those of notes in the Perfect System.
[3] Westphal, *die Musik*, p. 178, note.
[4] Cf. Archer-Hind, *op. cit.*, pp. 109, 110, note.

5

case, even if the scales are purely numerical scales, they seem to have been suggested by musical scales in actual use, and may be illustrated and explained by supposing them to be musical. We may safely see in the intervals between the terms of the series references to the ratios associated with musical intervals.

We have in Euclid's *sectio canonis* [1] the earliest statement in which the ratios [2] are explicitly given for the musical consonances. The first nine theorems (ten in Meibomius, *Antiquae Musicae Auctores Septem*) are purely mathematical, dealing with the ratios. In 10 (11 Meib.) the author proves that the interval διὰ πασῶν is multiple; in 11 (12) that the διὰ τεσσάρων and διὰ πέντε are each superparticular; in 12 (13–15) that the ratio of the διὰ πασῶν is 2 : 1, that the ratios of

---

[1] K. v. Jan, *Musici Scriptores Graeci*, p. 148, sq.

[2] A few words ought at this point to be said in explanation of the technical terms used in the arithmetic of the Greeks for various sorts of ratios. When the greater term of a ratio was compared with the lesser, and so usually preceded it, the ratio was called πρόλογος; when the lesser was compared with the greater, the ratio was called ὑπόλογος. There was also a distinction of three kinds of ratios according as the antecedent was greater than, was equal to, or was less than, the consequent, as in Theo Smyrnaeus, *de musica*, c. 22 (p. 74 Hiller): τῶν δὲ λόγων οἱ μέν εἰσι μείζονες, οἱ δὲ ἐλάττονες, οἱ δ'ἴσοι. Equal ratios are those in which the terms are equal. Of ratios where the first term is greater than the second, five kinds were distinguished: λόγοι πολλαπλάσιοι, λ. ἐπιμόριοι, λ. ἐπιμερεῖς, λ. πολλαπλασιεπιμόριοι, and λ. πολλαπλασιεπιμερεῖς. A *multiple* ratio is one whose first term contains the second an exact number of times (*op. cit.*, c. 23, p. 76, 8 Hiller); a *superparticular* ratio is one whose first term contains the second once and also an aliquot part of the second (c. 24, p. 76, 21); a *superpartient* ratio is one whose first term contains the second once and also more than one aliquot part of the second (c. 25, p. 78, 6); *multiplex-superparticular* (c. 26, p. 78, 23) and *multiplex-superpartient* (c. 27, p. 79, 15) ratios are like the last two kinds, but the first terms contain the second terms more than once, *plus* a fraction. Theon gives a sixth kind (*op. cit.*, c. 28, p. 80, 7), namely, λόγος ἀριθμοῦ πρὸς ἀριθμόν (found also in Ptolemy, *Harm.*, I. v., p. 10 Wallis). I do not see why this is not included under one of the other kinds. The example given is the ratio of 256 to 243, which is superpartient. The ὑπόλογοι have the same names as the πρόλογοι with the prefix ὑπο- added, as ὑποδιπλάσιος.

the διὰ πέντε and διὰ τεσσάρων are 3:2 and 4:3 respectively, that the ratio of the διὰ πέντε καὶ διὰ πασῶν is 3:1, and that the ratio of the δὶς διὰ πασῶν is 4:1. Theorems 13–16 (16–19) deal with the διάστημα τονιαῖον or τόνος, ratio 9:8, and show that the Octave is less than six Tones, and that the Fourth is less than two Tones and a Half-tone, and the Fifth than three Tones and a Half-tone. Theorem 16 shows that the Tone cannot be divided into two equal parts.[1] Since the proof is based on the fact that a superparticular ratio cannot be so divided, the same argument would show that the Fifth and the Fourth and other intervals with superparticular ratios are likewise indivisible into equal parts.

The Aristotelian *Problems*, even if they are not the work of Aristotle, are thought to be not much later in date than his time. The Nineteenth Section, entitled "Οσα περὶ ἁρμονίαν, contains a number of passages in which the interval ratios are mentioned. See problems 23, 34, 35, 39 b, 41, and 50 (p. 90, sq. K. v. Jan). The existence of the consonant ratios is affirmed (XIX. 39 b: οἱ ἐν τῇ συμφωνίᾳ φθόγγοι λόγον ἔχουσι κινήσεως πρὸς αὑτούς), and the ratios for the intervals of the Octave, Fifth, and Fourth are correctly given (35: διπλασία ἡ νήτη τῆς ὑπάτης, οἷα ἡ νήτη δύο, ἡ ὑπάτη ἕν, καὶ οἷα ἡ ὑπάτη δύο, ἡ νήτη τέσσαρα, καὶ ἀεὶ οὕτως· τῆς δὲ μέσης ἡμιολία. And 41: Διὰ τί δὶς μὲν δι' ὀξειῶν ἢ δὶς διὰ τεττάρων οὐ συμφωνεῖ, δὶς διὰ πασῶν δέ;—Ἡ ὅτι τὸ μὲν διὰ πέντε ἐστὶν ἐν ἡμιολίῳ λόγῳ, τὸ δὲ διὰ τεττάρων ἐν ἐπιτρίτῳ; .... τὸ δὲ διὰ πασῶν ἐπειδή ἐστιν ἐν διπλασίῳ λόγῳ, κτέ.).

Problems 23 and 50 describe experiments which show the ratios. Aristotle, *Problems*, XIX. 23 (p. 90 K. v. J.): Διὰ τί διπλασία τῆς νήτης ἡ ὑπάτη (ἡ νήτη τῆς ὑπάτης codd.);— Ἡ πρῶτον μὲν ὅτι ἐκ τοῦ ἡμίσεος ἡ χορδὴ ψαλλομένη καὶ ὅλη συμφωνοῦσι διὰ πασῶν. ὁμοίως δὲ ἔχει καὶ ἐπὶ τῶν συρίγγων. ἡ γὰρ διὰ τοῦ μέσου τῆς σύριγγος τρήματος φωνὴ τῇ δι' ὅλης τῆς σύριγγος συμφωνεῖ διὰ πασῶν. ἔτι ἐν τοῖς

---

[1] Cf. Archer-Hind, *loc. cit.*, p. 111, note (8).

αὐλοῖς τῷ διπλασίῳ διαστήματι λαμβάνεται τὸ διὰ πασῶν, καὶ οἱ αὐλοτρῦπαι οὕτω λαμβάνουσιν. καὶ οἱ τὰς σύριγγας ἁρμοττόμενοι εἰς μὲν τὴν ὑπάτην ἄκραν τὸν κηρὸν ἐμπλάττουσι, τὴν δὲ νήτην μέχρι τοῦ ἡμίσεος ἀναπληροῦσιν. ὁμοίως δὲ καὶ τὴν διὰ πέντε τῷ ἡμιολίῳ καὶ τὴν διὰ τεττάρων τῷ ἐπιτρίτῳ διαστήματι λαμβάνουσιν. ἔτι καὶ ἐν τοῖς τριγώνοις ψαλτηρίοις τῆς ἴσης ἐπιτάσεως γινομένης συμφωνοῦσι διὰ πασῶν ἡ μὲν διπλασία οὖσα ἡ δὲ ἡμίσεια τῷ μήκει. Ibid., 50 (p. 111 K. v. J.): Διὰ τί ἴσων πίθων καὶ ὁμοίων ἐὰν μὲν ὁ ἕτερος κενὸς ᾖ, ὁ δὲ ἕτερος εἰς τὸ ἥμισυ διάμεστος, διὰ πασῶν συμφωνεῖ ἡ ἠχώ;—Ἡ ὅτι διπλασία γίνεται ἡ ἐκ τοῦ ἡμίσεος τῆς ἐκ τοῦ κενοῦ; τί γὰρ διαφέρει τοῦτο ἢ ἐπὶ τῶν συρίγγων; δοκεῖ γὰρ ἡ θάττων κίνησις ὀξυτέρα εἶναι, ἐν δὲ τοῖς μείζοσι βραδύτερον ὁ ἀὴρ ἀπαντᾷ, καὶ ἐν τοῖς διπλασίοις τοσούτῳ καὶ ἐν τοῖς ἄλλοις ἀνάλογον. συμφωνεῖ δὲ διὰ πασῶν καὶ ὁ διπλασίων ἀσκὸς πρὸς τὸν ἥμισυν.

Theo Smyrnaeus devotes a number of paragraphs in his treatise de musica[1] to the ratios which are associated with the intervals. He gives the ratios of six consonant intervals and of the Tone and the Semitone or Diësis[2] (de mus., c. 12, p. 56, 9 Hiller), discovered by Pythagoras, by comparing the length and thickness of strings and their tension, as shown by the turning of the pegs or by hanging weights, and by comparing the bore of the cavities of wind-instruments and the force of the breath, and the masses and weights of sounding discs and vessels. It is then shown how the monochord (see above, p. 43) is employed to illustrate the consonant ratios (p. 57, 11 Hiller). The string is divided into 4 equal parts, of which 3 give a sound a Fourth above that given by the whole string, 2 (the half-string) give the Octave above, and 1 part gives the

---

[1] The de musica is the second of the three sections into which Theon's expositio rerum mathematicarum ad legendum Platonem utilium is divided. It covers pp. 46, 20—119, fin. in Hiller's edition (Teubner, 1878).

[2] The Pythagoreans called the Semitone both λεῖμμα and δίεσις, but the Aristoxeneans used the latter term for the Quarter-tone of the enharmonic genus. Cf. Theonem, loc. cit., p. 55 Hiller.

Double-octave, while 3 parts and 2 parts give the interval of the Fifth, and 3 parts and a single part give that of the Twelfth. All the consonances are embraced in the tetractys which consists of the four numbers, 1, 2, 3, and 4, because they give the necessary ratios (p. 58, 13 Hiller).

Theon next describes a number of experiments performed by some philosopher whose name does not appear in the manuscripts owing to the existence of a lacuna.[1] Vessels of the same size and shape are taken and the consonant intervals are produced by striking the vessels when filled with water to the proper heights.[2] Two strings are tuned in unison and one of them is shortened by being pressed against the finger-board at various points, with the result that the consonances are produced.[3] The same results are obtained from pan-pipes, and, it is stated, from weights attached to strings,[4] but, as we have noticed (p. 43), weights which produce a consonance will not give the ratio usually found, but the *duplicate ratio*. The stretching weights which produce any given interval must be to one another as the *squares* of the vibration-numbers of the

---

[1] See K. v. Jan., *Mus. Scr. Gr.*, p. 131.

[2] Theo Smyrn., *de mus.*, c. 12, p. 59, 12 Hiller : ἴσων γὰρ ὄντων καὶ ὁμοίων πάντων τῶν ἀγγείων τὸ μὲν κενὸν ἐάσας, τὸ δὲ ἥμισυ ὑγροῦ < πληρώσας > ἐψόφει ἑκατέρῳ, καὶ αὐτῷ ἡ διὰ πασῶν ἀπεδίδοτο συμφωνία· θάτερον δὲ πάλιν τῶν ἀγγείων κενὸν ἐῶν εἰς θάτερον τῶν τεσσάρων μερῶν τὸ ἓν ἐνέχεε, καὶ κρούσαντι αὐτῷ ἡ διὰ τεσσάρων συμφωνία ἀπεδίδοτο, ἡ δὲ διὰ πέντε, < ὅτε > ἓν μέρος τῶν τριῶν συνεπλήρου, οὔσης τῆς κενώσεως πρὸς τὴν ἑτέραν ἐν μὲν τῇ διὰ πασῶν ὡς β′ πρὸς ἕν, ἐν δὲ τῷ διὰ πέντε ὡς γ′ πρὸς β′, ἐν δὲ τῷ διὰ τεσσάρων ὡς δ′ πρὸς γ′.

[3] *Loc. cit.* continued : οἷς ὁμοίως καὶ κατὰ τὰς διαλήψεις τῶν χορδῶν θεωρεῖται, ὡς προείρηται, ἀλλ' οὐκ ἐπὶ μιᾶς χορδῆς, ὡς ἐπὶ τοῦ κανόνος, ἀλλ' ἐπὶ δυεῖν· δύο γὰρ ποιήσας ὁμοτόνους ὅτε μὲν τὴν μίαν αὐτῶν διαλάβοι μέσην πιέσας, τὸ ἥμισυ (p. 60) πρὸς τὴν ἑτέραν συμφωνίαν τὴν διὰ πασῶν ἐποίει· ὅτε δὲ τὸ τρίτον μέρος ἀπολαμβάνοι, τὰ λοιπὰ μέρη πρὸς τὴν ἑτέραν τὴν διὰ πέντε συμφωνίαν ἐποίει· ὁμοίως δὲ καὶ ἐπὶ τῆς διὰ τεσσάρων· καὶ γὰρ ἐπὶ ταύτης μιᾶς τῶν χορδῶν ἀπολαβὼν τὸ τέταρτον μέρος τὰ λοιπὰ μέρη πρὸς τὴν ἑτέραν συνῆπτεν.

[4] *Ibid.*, p. 60, 7 Hiller : οἱ δ' ἀπὸ τῶν βαρῶν τὰς συμφωνίας ἐλάμβανον, ἀπὸ δυεῖν χορδῶν ἐξαρτῶντες βάρη κατὰ τοὺς εἰρημένους λόγους.

notes.[1] Once again, it is possible to show the consonant ratios from the position of the finger-holes on flutes (αὐλοί).[2] The measurements are made from the mouth-piece downward.

In all of these experiments for determining the ratios, the correspondence between the ratios and the sensations is complete. In the words of the Peripatetic philosopher, Adrastus (Theo Smyrn., *de mus.*, c. 13, p. 61, 20 Hiller): τούτοις τοῖς εἰς τὴν ἀνεύρεσιν τῶν συμφωνιῶν ὀργάνοις κατὰ μὲν τοὺς λόγους προπαρασκευασθεῖσιν ἡ αἴσθησις ἐπιμαρτυρεῖ, τῇ δὲ αἰσθήσει προσληφθείσῃ ὁ λόγος ἐφαρμόζει. Not only do the consonances give the ratios, but the ratios give the consonances.

We have just noticed that the quaternion of the first four numbers, 1—2—3—4, is mentioned by Theon as containing all the consonant ratios. He returns to it at chapter 37 (p. 93, 17 Hiller), where it is called ἡ τῆς δεκάδος τετρακτύς, because the sum of the four terms is 10. They are, of course, in arithmetical progression. Theon next considers the two-branched quaternion of the *Timaeus*, in which the terms are in geometrical progression, and remarks in the course of his exposition that the ratios of the consonances are to be found in these terms.

This double quaternion seems to have been used by the Pythagoreans to illustrate various musical conceptions. We now turn to Plutarch's treatise *de animae procreatione in Timaeo Platonis*, c. 30, 1027 F, followed by c. 11, 1017 C, where the matter is discussed at considerable length.[3]

---

[1] Plutarch falls into this error in an interesting passage in the *de animae procreatione*. After giving the ratios of the consonant intervals, he says (c. 17, 1021 A): ἔξεστι δὲ καὶ νῦν βασανίσαι τἀληθές, ἢ βάρη δυεῖν ἄνισα χορδῶν ἐξαρτήσαντας ἢ δυεῖν ἰσοκοίλων αὐλῶν τὸν ἕτερον μήκει διπλάσιον τοῦ ἑτέρου ποιήσαντας· τῶν μὲν γὰρ αὐλῶν ὁ μείζων βαρύτερον φθέγξεται ὡς ὑπάτη πρὸς νήτην, τῶν δὲ χορδῶν ἡ τῷ διπλασίῳ κατατεινομένη βάρει τῆς ἑτέρας ὀξύτερον ὡς νήτη πρὸς ὑπάτην· τοῦτο δ' ἐστὶ διὰ πασῶν.

[2] Theo Smyrn., *de mus.*, c. 13, p. 60, 18, sq. Hiller: εἰ γοῦν κτέ.

[3] The passage = *Moralia*, VI. p. 181, sq., ed. Bernardakis (Teubner, 1895). For this order see Paul Tannery, *Revue des Études Grecques*, VII. p. 209.

After commenting on the wonderful properties of the Pythagorean tetractys, the number 36,[1] the author claims for the quaternion in question, called the Platonic tetractys, an even higher degree of perfection. The plan on which the quaternion is constructed is then set forth and the advantage of the Lambda-like arrangement is seen to be that like powers of 2 and 3 are conveniently placed for being added and multiplied together. In chapter 12 they are added: $2 + 3 = 5$; $4 + 9 = 13$; $8 + 27 = 35$; and the significance of these numbers is stated in the following words (Plut., de anim. procr., c. 12, 1017 F): τούτων γὰρ τῶν ἀριθμῶν οἱ Πυθαγορικοὶ τὰ μὲν ε′ τροφόν, ὅπερ ἐστὶ φθόγγον, ἐκάλουν, οἰόμενοι τῶν τοῦ τόνου διαστημάτων πρῶτον εἶναι φθεγκτὸν τὸ πέμπτον· τὰ δὲ τρισκαίδεκα λεῖμμα, καθάπερ Πλάτων, τὴν εἰς ἴσα τοῦ τόνου διανομὴν ἀπογιγνώσκοντες· τὰ δὲ πέντε καὶ τριάκοντα ἁρμονίαν, ὅτι συνέστηκεν ἐκ δυεῖν κύβων πρώτων ἀπ′ ἀρτίου καὶ περιττοῦ γεγονότων, ἐκ τεσσάρων δ′ ἀριθμῶν, τοῦ ϛ′ καὶ τοῦ η′ καὶ τοῦ θ′ καὶ ιβ′, τὴν ἀριθμητικὴν καὶ τὴν ἁρμονικὴν ἀναλογίαν περιεχόντων.

Nothing more is said at this place of 5, the τροφόν, and 13, the λεῖμμα,[2] but the nature of the ἁρμονία, 35, is illustrated by means of a diagram. A rectangle is constructed whose sides are to one another in length as 5 to 7. The area will then be 35. The author then divides the rectangle into four compartments by drawing two lines, one perpendicular to the shorter sides and dividing them each into two parts with lengths 2 and 3, and the other perpendicular to the longer sides and dividing them into parts with lengths 3 and 4.

---

[1] The sum of the first four even numbers and the first four odd numbers is 36:

$$1 + 3 + 5 + 7 = 16$$
$$\frac{2 + 4 + 6 + 8 = 20}{3 \quad 7 \quad 11 \quad 15 \quad 36}$$

Every odd number with the following even number forms a syzygy. The fourth syzygy, 7 and 8, is the first to form a square ($6^2 = 36$), whether alone or, as in the present case, added to the sum of its predecessors.

[2] The τροφόν will be discussed at p. 62, sq., the λεῖμμα at p. 57, sq.

The areas of the four compartments will then be 6, 8, 9, and 12 (sum, 35):

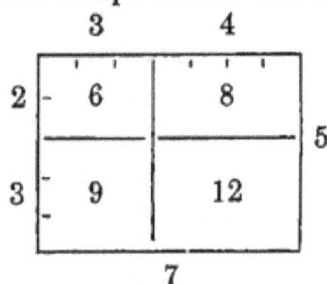

These numbers contain the arithmetical progression 6—9—12 and the harmonical progression 6—8—12; in the former we have the ratio of the Fifth (2:3) followed by that of the Fourth (3:4), in the latter, the order is reversed, while the ratio of the extremes is that of the Octave (1:2), and the ratio of the two means is that of the Tone (8:9). Διὰ τοῦτο καὶ ἁρμονίαν τὸν περιέχοντα τοὺς λόγους τούτους ἀριθμὸν ἐκάλεσαν (loc. cit., 1018 B). The musical notes corresponding to these numbers are: ὑπάτη—μέση—παραμέση—νήτη, the intervals between them being Fourth, Tone, Fourth.[1]

Plutarch next multiplies like powers of 2 and 3 (chapter 13, 1018 B, sq.). The products, 6, 36, and 216, are, of course, the first, second, and third powers of 6. In commenting on these numbers, the remark is made that 36 is the smallest number which is at once a square and a triangle, for it is the square of 6 and the triangle[2] of 8 (τρίγωνος ἀπὸ τῆς

---

[1] This Pythagorean 'harmony' of four notes is supposed to have been discovered by the philosopher on his famous visit to the smithy, when he noticed that the hammers used gave notes which formed the various consonances. On returning home, it is said, he fastened weights proportional to those of the hammers to four strings of equal length, and thus obtained the four notes of the harmony. Cf. Iamblichus, Life of Pythagoras, XXVI. (117) sq.; Plutarch, de musica, c. 22, 1138 C, sq.; c. 23, 1139 B, sq. The four notes stand at the same intervals from one another as do the tonic, subdominant, dominant, and tonic again, in modern music. The arithmetical progression gives the dominant, and the harmonical progression (so called for this reason) gives the subdominant.

[2] On triangular numbers, see Theo Smyrn., de rebus math. etc., p. 33 Hiller (= de arithmetica, c. 19), and p. 37, 7, sq. (c. 23). The number in question, 36, is the sum of 1, 2, 3, 4, 5, 6, 7, and 8.

ὀγδοάδος); and that it is the product of two squares (4 × 9 = 36) and the sum of three cubes (1 + 8 + 27 = 36). Moreover it forms two parallelograms, one 3 by 12, the other 4 by 9. If now (1018 D) we take 6 (the side of the square) and 8 (the side of the triangle) and 9 and 12 (sides of the two parallelograms), we have in these numbers the ratios of the consonances.

There are a number of passages in the following chapters of the *de animae procreatione* in which the consonant ratios are given, but they are not important enough to be quoted, being for the most part but repetitions of former statements. But a few words should be said in regard to the two dissonant intervals, the Tone and the Leimma, which are closely connected with the consonances. We have already remarked (p. 46) that the Tone (*i. e.*, the Major Whole-tone, ratio 8 : 9) owes its prominence largely to the fact that it is the difference in width of the Fifth and the Fourth; and the Leimma is important in the formation of certain scales (for example, the scales in the *Timaeus*), owing to the fact that it is the interval which must be added to two and to three Tones to make the Fourth and the Fifth respectively.

The Pythagoreans associated two numbers with these intervals, 13 with the Leimma,[1] and 27 with the Tone. It is easily seen that these numbers express approximately the relative size of the intervals, for the Fourth is a little less than two Tones and a half, so that the Leimma is a little less than an exact Semitone. The method of obtaining these numbers will now be given.

In regard to the Leimma, the number is derived directly from the ratio 243 : 256 (which we obtain by dividing the ratio of the Fourth by that of the Ditone, or Pythagorean Third (= two Tones), as follows: $\frac{3}{4} \div \frac{8^1}{9^1} = \frac{3}{4} \times \frac{81}{64} = \frac{243}{256}$), and is nothing more nor less than the arithmetical difference between the two terms.

It is, of course, illogical to identify an interval with the absolute difference of two numbers which express its ratio.

[1] See the quotation from Plutarch on p. 55.

This arithmetical difference varies with the size of the terms which compose the ratio, whereas the size of the ratio is independent of the size of the terms used in forming it. For example, the Fifth is expressed by any of the following ratios, 2 : 3, 6 : 9, 100 : 150, but the difference is now 1, now 3, now 50. But there is this to be said, that whereas the ratios of most of the intervals occurring in music are reducible to ratios whose arithmetical difference is 1, or occasionally 2, the ratio of the Leimma cannot be reduced to any lower terms than 243 : 256, and the difference will therefore always be either 13 or a multiple of 13.

To show how 27 could be regarded as representing the size of the Tone, we must turn again to the scales in the *Timaeus* constructed on the double geometrical quaternion. When the duple and triple intervals which characterize the two branches are filled up with arithmetical and harmonical means, the series obtained involve fractional numbers (see the series given on p. 48), and when every epitrite ratio (3 : 4) is filled up with epogdoa (8 : 9), as far as possible, leaving Leimmata, the new terms to be inserted necessitate the use of inconveniently large numbers in expressing the improper fractions which result. To avoid these fractions, we may follow the example of the ancient commentators, and multiply all the terms of the series by the same number, so as to obtain whole numbers alone in which to express the ratios. The first four terms of the binary branch, 1, $\frac{4}{3}$, $\frac{3}{2}$, 2, become 6, 8, 9, 12, when multiplied by the least common multiple of the denominators of the fractions. If now we take the first interval in the series, the ratio 3 : 4, and proceed to insert two intervals of 8 : 9, we must multiply the terms of the ratio by 8^2. This gives $3 \times 8^2 : 4 \times 8^2 =$ 192 : 256, and we have the following series after inserting the epogdoa : 192 (Tone) 216 (Tone) 243 (Leimma) 256; and if we take the arithmetical differences, we obtain :

for the Leimma, $256 - 243 = 13$,

and for the two Tones, $243 - 216 = 27$,

and $216 - 192 = 24$.

59

The number 27 is, then, derived from the numbers 216 and 243, used to express the ratio of the Tone which stands next to the Leimma when whole numbers are used to illustrate the diatonic division of the tetrachord (Fourth) used in the scales of the *Timaeus*.

The series given above is found in a number of the commentaries on the double quaternion (*e. g.*, Theo Smyrnaeus, *de mus.*, c. 14, p. 67, 16, sq. Hiller; Plutarch, *de anim. procr.*, c. 18, 1021 E, sq.; Nicomachus, *excerpta*, 2, p. 30 Meib. (p. 267 K. v. J.)),[1] and is sufficient when a single tetrachord is under consideration. But when a whole Octave of the binary scale is expressed in whole numbers and the second Leimma appears, it is necessary to double the numbers which make up the series. This gives: 384 (Tone) 432 (Tone) 486 (Leimma) 512[2] for the first tetrachord. Theon gives this series (*loc. cit.*, p. 68, 12, sq. Hiller), and mentions the objection to it that it does not give the ratio given by Plato for the Leimma, 243 : 256, with its difference 13; but, as he truly remarks, the ratio of the Leimma may be expressed in other numbers, as 486 : 512. Chapter 16 of Plutarch's *de anim. procr.* (1019 E, sq.) gives the process by which these numbers are obtained. If 384 is taken for the first term of the binary and ternary scales, all the following terms in both the branches can be expressed in whole numbers.[3]

---

[1] In Plato small numbers represent acute sounds, and the scales run downward from unity, so that the Leimmata are at the grave end of the tetrachords; but in Plutarch and Nicomachus the reverse is the case, and the Leimma in each tetrachord stands above the Tones (Plut., *loc. cit.*, 1021 F: τοῦ γὰρ βαρυτέρου τόνῳ ἐπιταθέντος, ὅπερ ἐστὶν ἐπόγδοον, γίγνεται σις'· τούτου πάλιν τόνῳ ἄλλῳ ἐπιταθέντος, γίγνεται σμγ'. . . . . (1022 A) περίεστι τοῦ ὅλου διάστημα λοιπὸν τὸ μεταξὺ τῶν σμγ' καὶ τῶν σνς', τὰ τρισκαίδεκα· διὸ καὶ λεῖμμα τοῦτον τὸν ἀριθμὸν ὠνόμαζον. Nicom., *loc. cit.*, ἐπιτείνουσι). The same set of figures can illustrate these two situations according as they stand for length of string or for vibration numbers. Cf. Theonem Smyrnaeum, p. 65, 10 Hiller.

[2] The whole series is: 384—432—486—512—576—648—729—768.

[3] See Boeckh, *Kleine Schriften*, III. *Ueber die Bildung der Weltseele im Timaeos des Platon*, p. 76 (p. 158), sq.

Still another series is given in Plutarch, *de anim. procr.*, c. 19, 1026 A, to show the division of the Fourth when the Leimma is the middle of the three intervals. It is:

216 (Tone) 243 (Leimma) 256 (Tone) 288

differences :   27   13   32

From these figures it is proved that the Leimma is less than half a Tone, for 13 is less than one-half of either 27 or 32. The same conclusion is reached at c. 14, 1018 E, where we read : καὶ τῶν ἐμμελῶν διαστημάτων οἱ Πυθαγορικοὶ τὸν τόνον ἐν τούτῳ τῷ ἀριθμῷ [*i.e.* 27] τάττουσι· διὸ καὶ τὰ τρισκαίδεκα λεῖμμα καλοῦσιν· ἀπολείπει γὰρ μονάδι τοῦ ἡμίσεος.[1]

Inasmuch as the Leimma was the lowest of the three intervals into which every Fourth between ‘standing’ notes[2] was divided to form the ‘high-pitched’ variety of the diatonic *genus* (διάτονον σύντονον, or rather διάτονον διτονιαῖον), the numbers given above[3] for this tetrachord can be conveniently used to give a practical illustration of the size of the intervals concerned, because they may be regarded as representing lengths of string.[4] In this we may imagine ourselves to be repeating

---

[1] The same derivation for the term λεῖμμα (that it is an imperfect or short Semitone) is given at c. 17, 1020 F (p. 194, 22 Bernardakis): λεῖμμα τὸ ἔλαττον ὀνομάζουσιν, ὅτι τοῦ ἡμίσεος ἀπολείπει; Gaudentius, *harm. introd.*, 14, p. 16 Meib. (p. 343 K. v. J.). Other writers seem to derive the term from the fact that the λεῖμμα is the interval left when two Tones have been taken from the Fourth (or three from the Fifth), as Nicomachus, *excerpta*, 2, p. 30, sq. Meib. (pp. 267–271 K. v. J., *passim*): τὸ καταλειπόμενον λεῖμμα. τὰ λειπόμενά εἰσι λθ′ (39 = 3 × 13). λείπεται ὁ ιγ′. καταλειπόμενα ἔσται ιγ′. διαλείπει νβ′ (52 = 4 × 13); see too Plutarch, *de anim. procr.*, c. 18, 1022 A (p. 197, 24 Bern.), quoted above, p. 59, n¹. The following passage brings out the fact that it is in constituting the perfect Fourth with Tones that the λεῖμμα is needed and on examination turns out to be a short Half-tone and so a blemish to the Fourth: Theo Smyrnaeus, *de mus.*, c. 15, p. 70, 3 Hiller: τὸ δὲ λεγόμενον λεῖμμα εἴ τις ἐρωτῴη τίνος ἐστὶ λεῖμμα, δεῖ εἰδέναι ὅτι ἐστὶ τοῦ διὰ τεσσάρων· τῷ [? τὸ] γὰρ διὰ τεσσάρων λείπει πρὸς τὸ γενέσθαι δύο ἥμισυ τόνων τελείων.

[2] Φθόγγοι ἑστῶτες are those notes which keep the same pitch in all three of the *genera*, the diatonic, chromatic, and enharmonic. They form the frame-work, as it were, of the scales.

[3] P. 58, *viz.*: 192—216—243—256.   [4] Cf. p. 59, n¹.

the experiment of some ancient investigator. Let the sound produced by the whole length of a string be the lowest of two notes forming a Fourth. The upper note will then be given by three-quarters of the string. In order to descend by Major-tones from this upper note, it is necessary twice in succession to increase the length of the vibrating part of the string by an eighth part of itself. The $\frac{3}{4}$ of the string must, then, be multiplied by $\frac{9}{8}$ to give the length which will sound the second (descending) note, and the result by $\frac{9}{8}$ again to give the third. We shall have $\frac{3}{4} \times \frac{9}{8} \times \frac{9}{8} = \frac{243}{256}$ for the length used for this third (next to the gravest) note. Therefore, if the whole string is divided into 256 equal parts, when the string is 'stopped' by the finger so as to cut off 13 parts (leaving 243 to vibrate), it will give a note forming with the open string the interval of the Leimma. The next 27 parts (making 40) will give a note acuter than the last by the interval of a Tone, and the next 24 (making 64 in all) will give another Tone, completing the whole Fourth. In this way the Pythagorean numerical values for the Tone and Leimma may be practically illustrated.

We have now seen how the Pythagoreans put a musical interpretation on the sum of the *squares* of 2 and 3 and on the sum of their *cubes*, the numbers of the double quaternion having been arranged in the convenient form of a Lambda, which suggested the idea of adding like powers. On the one hand, they took the result of the addition (the number 35, the sum of the cubes), made a new separation of the material, and obtained, as the result of the analysis, four numbers (6, 8, 9, and 12), such that they can represent the four most important notes of the octachord of Pythagoras (hypatê, mesê, paramesê, and nêtê [1]), whether they are regarded

---

[1] They are the 'standing' notes (see p. 60, n², above). In the (Greater) Perfect System (which is the original octachord expanded at each end) their names are: ὑπάτη μεσῶν, μέση, παραμέση, and νήτη διεζευγμένων (νήτων). See Müller's *Handbuch* (2nd revised ed.), II. E. e. (*Die Musik der Griechen*, by H. Gleditsch), § 200, pp. 860–862.

as proportional to the lengths of the vibrating strings or, in modern manner, to the vibration-numbers of the notes.[1] On the other hand, they connected the result (13, the sum of the squares) with a particular ratio, which they used to express a certain interval occurring in their scales. The fact that the numbers concerned in these operations can be dealt with in this way is the merest coincidence. It is nothing more than an arithmetical accident (to call it such) that the sum of the squares should equal the difference between 256 and 243, or that the sum of the cubes should also be the sum of 6, 8, 9, and 12, numbers in which an arithmetical and an harmonical progression can be found. But such is the state of affairs.

It remains that we should consider the sum of the *first powers*, the number 5, which the Pythagoreans called τροφόν, according to the passage from Plutarch quoted on p. 55. So far as I am aware, no explanation has ever been given for this number, beyond what is contained in Plutarch's words. They are (*de anim. procr.*, c. 12, 1017 F): οἱ Πυθαγορικοὶ τὰ μὲν ε′ τροφόν, ὅπερ ἐστὶ φθόγγον, ἐκάλουν, οἰόμενοι τῶν τοῦ τόνου διαστημάτων πρῶτον εἶναι φθεγκτὸν τὸ πέμπτον. The following seems to me to be the solution of the problem. Using the same apparatus as we had in the experiment just described, if we measure off 5 of the 256 equal parts and stop the string at that point, we obtain a small interval about a third of a Semitone in size.[2] This interval I believe to

---

[1] It is immaterial whether we run up the scale or down, since the three intervals are *symmetrically* arranged (an epitrite ratio on either side of the epogdoön).

[2] An idea of the width of this interval may be gained without the trouble of dividing a string into 256 parts. After sounding the open string of an instrument like the violin, play as accurately as possible, by ear, a note at the interval of a Semitone to the acute, by pressing on the string with the finger; divide the piece of string cut off for the Semitone into three equal parts; then press down the first of the three (that nearest the end of the string), so as to keep it from vibrating. The remaining string will give a note acuter than the open string by the interval in question. Since our 'natural' Semitone is slightly larger than the Pythagorean Leimma

be the τροφόν, and that the Pythagoreans hit on this as an explanation for the number 5 from the following considerations. The interval is so small that the difference in the two pitches is but little, if any, wider than those differences in pitch which make a note out of tune to the average ear. That is, it is about the smallest interval which differs sufficiently from unison to be entitled to the designation 'musical interval.' We feel a natural reluctance to calling minute pitch-differences by the same name as those evident alterations of pitch on which music is based. In considering the effect of cutting off the small divisions one after the other experimenters may easily have come to the conclusion that the first of the 256 parts (apparently called 'intervals of the tone,' but for what reason we can only surmise, for the phrase does not occur elsewhere as far as I am aware) makes no interval 'which can be sounded' (φθεγκτόν), nor does the second, nor the third, nor the fourth, but the fifth gives a note which can be regarded as forming a distinct interval with the open string. The passage will then run: "The Pythagoreans called *five* τροφόν ['food' apparently [1]]—that is a (musical)

($\frac{1}{1} = \frac{1}{1} \times \frac{1}{1}$), it is probable that about 15 of the 256 parts would be taken (16 would be the exact number to take) for sounding the Semitone, instead of the 13 required for the Leimma; consequently a third of them would fall very near to the 5 which form the desired interval.

[1] In the above I have regarded τροφόν as the accusative of the neuter form τὸ τροφόν, meaning 'food, nourishment' which occurs in Plato, *Polit.*, 289 A. It has been suggested to me that we may have here the accusative of the commoner masculine and feminine τροφός 'feeder, nourisher, nurse,' that the number 5 is personified after a fashion characteristic of the Pythagoreans. For example 7 was called 'Αθηνᾶ and παρθένος, because alone among the numbers which compose the decade, 7 neither generates nor is generated, that is, it is neither a factor nor a multiple of any other number in the decade (cf. Theon. Smyrn., *de mus.*, c. 46, p. 103 Hiller). Somewhat similarly 5 was sometimes called γάμος because it can be regarded as the union or marriage of the first odd number, 3, which is male, with the first even number, 2, which is female (1 is a number apart). The thought would then seem to be that 5 plays the rôle of a nurse in bringing out the first sound which is φθεγκτόν.

sound—on the supposition that of the intervals of the tone the fifth is the first which can be sounded." In support of this theory of the musical signification of 5 we have the parallel cases of the numbers 13 and 27, whose connection with musical intervals arises, as we have seen, from the terms of the ratios (expressing their size) derived from the monochord with a scale of 256 equal divisions. The three numbers, 5, 13, and 27, are then (not quite exactly) proportional to the sizes of the intervals, the τροφόν, the λεῖμμα, and the Tone, since they are all three measured on the same scale. The Pythagorean τροφόν is then, I take it, a small interval with the ratio 251 : 256, and was connected with the number 5, because 5 is the arithmetical difference between the terms of the ratio, just as 13 and 27 are arithmetical differences.[1]

In the foregoing pages we have cited and discussed some of the more important passages in which the ratios of the primary consonances are either established or assumed as known, with the object of showing that the ancients were thoroughly familiar with the numerical relations which exist between musical notes, and that they made free use of the resulting ratios in measuring the size of intervals. A considerable number of additional passages could be adduced, were it necessary in a matter which is often taken for granted. Moreover, it is not necessary in the case of the consonant intervals to examine closely the value of the experiments by

---

[1] In the explanation given above,—that it is only when the minute interval corresponding to the fifth of the 256 equal parts of a vibrating string is joined to the four which preceded that a 'soundable' interval is obtained, and that 5 stands for this interval,—it is not a serious objection that the writer first calls 5 a φθόγγος and then seems to identify it with an interval. The confusion between a note and the interval which it forms with some given note is of frequent occurrence; each new sound brings in a new interval, i. e. with the open string. The difficulty can, however, be removed by changing φθόγγον to φθόγγου or φθόγγων. If φθόγγον is kept, can it be that ψόφον should be read for τροφόν? The clause ὅπερ ἐστὶ φθόγγον would seem to support this emendation in view of the fact that φθόγγος and ψόφος were not always carefully differentiated.

means of which the aucients made their original determinations of these ratios, inasmuch as the true ratio of a consonance could have been derived,[1] and as a matter of fact
must have been derived in the first instance, from imperfect
observations by a sort of intuitive preference for simple
ratios. But when one comes to the consideration of the
numerous divisions of the tetrachord according to *genus* and
chroa (color), in which Greek musical theory abounded, it
becomes important to ascertain whether the measurements
given for these dissonant intervals by the method of ratios
are to be trusted as true indications of their size. Many of
these intervals are so utterly foreign to modern European
music that it is difficult to believe that they were actually of
the width ascribed to them. We refer to such intervals as
the Quarter-tones in the enharmonic *genus*, the intervals of
three-quarters and five-quarters of a Tone in the διάτονον
μαλακόν, and the intervals in the χρῶμα μαλακόν and
χρῶμα ἡμιόλιον.

The degree of accuracy attainable in measuring the size of
any interval depends upon several considerations. In the
first place intervals differ vastly among themselves in the
exactness with which they may be tuned.[2] Variations may
be due to the failure of the experimenters to obtain uniformly
the ideal intonation of the interval. In the next place intervals of nearly the same size are apt to be confounded. We
have already alluded to the fact that in modern music the
interval known to musicians as the Tone is not an interval of
fixed width. In the same way the term Semitone is used now

---

[1] A. J. Ellis is unwilling to give the ancients credit for accuracy in these
measurements. He says (Helmholtz, *Sensations of Tone*, 2nd Eng. ed., p. 15,
note *): "As the monochord is very liable to error, these results were happy
generalisations from necessarily imperfect experiments." But Helmholtz
says (*op. cit.*, p. 14): "These measurements had been executed with great
precision by the Greek musicians, and had given rise to a system of tones,
contrived with considerable art."

[2] "Distinctness of delimitation." Helmholtz-Ellis, *op. cit.*

for this intervallar width and now for that, whether conscious-
ness of these differences exist or not. If the existence of the
small but real difference is unknown to the experimenters, an
apparently variable character will be imparted to the interval
supposed to be undergoing measurement, resulting in discrep-
ancies in the magnitudes assigned to it by different observers.
We must be assured that we are in fact dealing with only a
single difference of pitch and not with two or more. Lastly
we must take into account the imperfections of the instrument
on which the measurements are made. Within what limits
are errors due to the instruments confined? If now the width
of an ancient interval is given by a certain ratio, these points
must be taken into consideration. We must ask, Was the
interval such that musicians could tune the notes forming it
so as to give invariably the same width? Was there no
neighboring interval with which it could be confounded? and
then, How accurately was it possible with the existing instruments to measure the interval *when tuned?*

Leaving the accuracy of the measuring instruments aside
for the present, as a matter in regard to which we have but
little direct knowledge, if we turn to consider the nature of
the intervals, we notice immediately this striking difference
between consonant and dissonant intervals, that the former
can be tuned with a high degree of precision, while in the
case of the latter there is a far greater range within which the
size of the interval may vary without attracting attention.
It is well known that small errors in the intonation of the
more dissonant intervals are more readily overlooked than
are errors of the same size in the case of mistuned consonances. The reason for this is that the consonant intervals
are bounded on all sides by harsh discords—harsher discords
exist only among the small intervals which stand next to
unison. For example, if the Octave be made a little too
large or a little too small, the result is a painfully dissonant
interval, and the same holds true in the case of the other
consonances, when put slightly out of tune. It follows that

these intervals were tuned with a far greater degree of accuracy than was possible in the case of the dissonant intervals. The consonant intervals at least were fixed in point of size. That is to say, we may be sure that all the ancient philosophers who undertook to measure the size of the διὰ πασῶν, διὰ πέντε, and the other consonances were measuring exactly the same magnitudes in all cases, and that these magnitudes are the same as the pitch-differences which we call Octave, Fifth, etc. But there is no discrepancy in the reported ratios for these intervals. We are not told by one that the ratio for the Octave is 50 : 100, by another that it is 50 : 101. We are led to conclude either that the defects in the instruments used for the finer measurements were not serious, or that the ancient theorists were so impressed with the necessity that the perfect consonances should have the simpler and more perfect ratios as to persist in ignoring inconvenient variations in the results, even while they discoursed of intervals which differed in size by only the twelfth of a Semitone. The first alternative seems preferable. For if the Greek monochord was accurate enough to allow experimenters to distinguish between intervals which differed by only this small amount, then their measurements for the Fourth, for instance, cannot have been wrong by an amount equal to or greater than that difference, unless we suppose them to be so dishonest as to suppress its existence.

It would accordingly seem to follow that we must ascribe the same degree of accuracy to the measurements of dissonant intervals as to those of the consonances, so far as concerns the determination of their size *after they have been tuned*. If it is reported on good authority that the size of a certain interval is given by a certain ratio, we are not at liberty to ignore this evidence, and no matter how unusual the interval may seem to our ears when it is produced mechanically from the ratio, we must concede that the interval intended by the ancient theorist cannot have differed appreciably from the interval thus reproduced.

We have then in the ratios a trustworthy means of identifying ancient Greek intervals with their modern equivalents and of realizing the size of those intervals which are not recognized in our modern European system. We are forced to seek other causes for the great number of dissonant intervals which we find in the theory of Greek music than supposed defects in the instruments of measurement.

We have already seen that the facility with which the consonant intervals may be accurately tuned, or perhaps it would be better to say the artistic necessity to tune them accurately, is a guarantee that any fluctuations in their measured size are due to the measurements and not to any variations in their real size, and that, since no such fluctuations are recorded even when the experimenters professed to make the finest of distinctions, it is reasonable to conclude that all the measurements were made with the degree of care and precision claimed for them. The other side of this characteristic difference between consonant and dissonant intervals is the difficulty of tuning the latter with precision and the absence of any necessity for great precision. This we consider to have been a much more fertile cause of variations in their recorded size than any impossibility of eliminating errors due to the measuring apparatus. In the case of instruments which require frequent tuning, such as the lyre and other stringed instruments, much evidently depends on the ear for pitch-differences of the individual performer. In the case of instruments whose tones are fixed in pitch at the time of manufacture, like the αὐλός and fingered stringed instruments when their tones depend on fixed frets along the finger-board, the same personal element enters in the (original) tuning of the instrument, and is complicated by the fact that the pitch of the notes could be regulated during the performance by the force of the breath in the case of wind-instruments and by pressure on the string behind the frets of fingered stringed instruments, and in other ways. And in vocal music this difficulty of tuning notes at dissonant intervals from one

another is evidently at its maximum, except as it is lessened
by the restraining influence of accompanying instruments.

This enables us to reduce the number of intervals which
had a distinct and separate existence by merging into one all
those intervals which are so nearly of a size that we are
justified in regarding them as different aspects of the same
phenomenon. But after we have carried this process as far as
it is reasonable to do so, the number of intervals left is still
very great—far greater than we admit in modern theory.
Many of them are irreconcilably different in width. These
intervals, it would seem, must be accepted as having an independent existence and as being necessary to the formation of
the scales of Greek music. But it is not necessary to assume
that they all existed in actual music at the same time. There
is still another possible cause for the differences in the size of
intervals which must be considered in any attempt to appreciate the scales of Greek music, and with it we bring our
discussion to a conclusion.

It is the liability to which dissonant intervals in particular,
if not alone, are subject of undergoing a gradual change in
their size with the development of the scale of which they are
a part. It must be borne in mind that homophonic or pure
melodic music [1] does not demand a strict adherence to definite
degrees of pitch in the formation of its scales, and variation
in the width of the intervals is necessarily a result of this
freedom. In considering variations due to the tuning we
assumed an ideal intonation for the interval which the best
authorities would recognize as a just intonation. In the case
of the variations now under consideration there is no criterion
by which it is possible to select one width in preference to
another as a more perfect representative of the interval.
Fixed degrees of pitch come in with simultaneous harmony,
of which we know that Greek music made little use. When

---

[1] Parry says (*Art of Music*, p. 19): " Purely melodic schemes " "only
admit of a single line of tune at a time."

two notes are sounded together it is instinctive to avoid as much as possible the roughness produced by rapid beats between nearly coincident partials and combinational tones,[1] and this results in a tendency to make the intervals true— i. e., true to those vibration-numbers which will give the fewest beats or none at all—and so to fix the width of the intervals according to the simpler ratios, because they give the best results. Every note in our modern scale has had its just intonation (not, of course, its tempered intonation) fixed by these very considerations,[2] for every one of them is used on occasion as part of a chord. Now in Greek music the designation 'consonant interval' was limited to the Octave, Fifth, and Fourth, and those intervals which are equal to one of these *plus* one or more Octaves (cf. p. 45). Music was not ready to take the step by which Thirds and Sixths were recognized as consonant. As a result, all dissonant intervals, except possibly those which are derived from the consonances by subtraction, such as the Major-tone and the Leimma (cf. p. 57), were free from any such influence (and it is a powerful influence) tending to fix their size permanently. The consonant intervals may have been tuned (the probabilities are strong that they were always tuned) by sounding the notes simultaneously, but it is not likely that the Greek dissonances could have gained anything in exactness of tuning from sounding the notes together.[3] It would accordingly not be

---

[1] That is, to avoid *dissonance*, as defined by Helmholtz, *op. cit.*, 2nd Eng. ed. by Ellis, p. 194.

[2] Helmholtz, *op. cit.*, Pt. II., Ch. X., p. 179, last lines: "These beats play a principal part in settling the consonant intervals of our musical scales." Parry, *op. cit.*, p. 19: "Our scale has had to be transformed entirely from the ancient modes in order to make the harmonic scheme of æsthetics possible."

[3] Cf. Plutarch, *de anim. procr.*, c. 17, 1021 B (this passage follows closely on that quoted at p. 54, note [1], above): ἐὰν δ' ὡς ἐννέα πρὸς ὀκτὼ γένηται τῶν βαρῶν ἢ τῶν μηκῶν ἡ ἀνισότης, ποιήσει διάστημα τονιαῖον οὐ σύμφωνον ἀλλ' ἐμμελὲς ὡς εἰπεῖν ἔμβραχυ, τῷ τοὺς φθόγγους, ἂν ἀνὰ μέρος κρουσθῶσι, παρέχειν ἡδὺ φωνοῦντας καὶ προσηνές· ἂν δ' ὁμοῦ, τραχὺ καὶ λυπηρόν· ἐν δὲ ταῖς συμφωνίαις κἂν ὁμοῦ κρούωνται κἂν ἐναλλάξ, ἡδέως προσίεται τὴν συνήχησιν ἡ αἴσθησις.

surprising if it could be shown that the dissonant intervals
varied in size with the history of Greek music, and that this
variation manifested itself in the various ratios which different philosophers obtained for intervals which bore the same
name. We must admit the existence of the host of dissonant
intervals and explain them, not as the result of theoretic
speculations, without basis in fact, on the part of the ancient
writers on the theory of music, but as proof of real variations
in the pitch of the notes, and then endeavor to account for
these variations, when not attributable to imperfections in the
tuning, as due to influences which we cannot trace which in
process of time wrought gradual changes in the intonation of
the notes as actually sung and played.

———————————

INDEX OF PASSAGES QUOTED OR REFERRED TO.

GENERAL INDEX.

CORRIGENDA.

P. 2, l. 22: *for* works *read* words.

P. 7, n.[3]: *for* XI. 14, *read* XI. 35; *and for* 35 *read* 14.

P. 7, n.[4]: *for* p. 51 *read* pp. 55, 137. Cf. p. 51.

P. 8, ll. 29–31 : *omit.*

P. 9, l. 18: *read:* Ψόφος δὲ πάθος ἀέρος πλησσομένου, τὸ πρῶτον καὶ γενικώτατον τῶν ἀκουστῶν.

P. 19, l. 7 : *after* ὅταν *add* μὲν.

P. 28, ll. 33, 34: *for* κεκλᾶσθαι *and* κλᾶσιν *read* κεκλάσθαι *and* κλάσιν.

P. 39, l. 25: The investigations of R. G. Kiesewetter and of J. P. N. Land have shown that the opinion previously held by European writers that the 17 intervals of the Arabic scale were equal or nearly so was wrong (see Helmholtz-Ellis, *Sensations of Tone,* 2nd Eng. ed., p. 281 sq., and notes, and p. 520). This Arabic scale cannot therefore be used in the argument. We may substitute the Javese scale in which the Octave seems to be divided into 5 nearly equal intervals (see Ellis, *op. cit.,* pp. 518 and 522 (nos. 94, 95)).

www.ingramcontent.com/pod-product-compliance
Lightning Source LLC
Chambersburg PA
CBHW031454270326
41930CB00007B/999

*9 7 8 3 7 4 4 7 4 3 2 5 9 *